Small Houses
Nicolas Pople

Laurence King
Publishing

Small Houses
Nicolas Pople

To Laura, James and Søren
Pople, who knew what was
important when they were small,
and were wise enough not to
forget it when they grew up.

LAURENCE KING

Published in 2003 by
Laurence King Publishing
71 Great Russell Street
London WC1B 3BP
United Kingdom
Tel: +44 20 7430 8850
Fux: +44 20 7430 8880
e-mail: enquiries@laurenceking.co.uk
www.laurenceking.co.uk

A catalogue record for this book is
available from the British Library.

ISBN 1 85669 296 5

Designed by Rose Design, London
Picture research by Jennifer Hudson
Printed in Singapore

Frontispiece: Little House, Vilches, Talca, Chile,
1995, Smilijan Radic.

Pages 6-7: Think Tank Boathouse,
Skibbereen, Ireland, 1998, Philip
Gumuchdijan.

Contents

'Difficult things in the world must needs have their beginnings in the easy; big things must needs have their beginnings in the small.'

Lao Tzu, Founder of Taoism, c.500 BC

The small house is the most recent in the panoply of clearly identifiable building types – which gives rise to a paradox: the small house is both the first building in human history and the one with the shortest record in terms of architectural history. However, if architecture is seen as a conscious process in which ideas, abstractions and received theories inform the practice of building, then the earliest architecture belonged to the realm of the sacred, devoted as it was to sites of worship, ritual and recognition of the divine. Art and architecture reflect human evolution, and this first architecture – manifested through monumental structures and buildings to house gods rather than people – illustrates a complete lack of human individualization or self-awareness.

In On Adam's House in Paradise, Joseph Rykwert quotes Jean Jacques Rousseau's account of the process of human detachment from this mythic state of grace and innocence:[1] 'Here

is a calm riverbank, dressed by the hand of unaided nature, towards which the eye turns constantly, and which you leave with regret. Here at a time when innocent and virtuous men wanted the gods to witness their actions, they lived together with them in the same huts. But soon men turned wicked, tired of embarrassing onlookers, and relegated them to magnificent temples. Finally men chased the gods out altogether, so as to inhabit those temples themselves: or at any rate, the temples of the gods came to look very much like citizens' houses.'

Rousseau is describing the emergence of individual human consciousness and imagination, a continuing process that has its roots in prehistory, and its clear manifestation in modern times, when many cohesive belief systems are breaking down. We are living in a period where the temple has become the house, and the small house – the kind of house which

most of us by necessity inhabit – will receive more and more attention as a design issue. This book is a review of some of the best examples of small houses built worldwide within the past decade.

In any historical epoch the way we build houses reflects how we see ourselves as part of the world – houses are our second bodies. In ancient times there was no sense of the private person, and therefore the house as a reflection of self was not important; it was the body of the community or the city that mattered. In the Egyptian period, the function of the temple was to initiate human beings into the mysteries of their own physical bodies. R. A. Schwaller de Lubicz, specifically in his research work of about 1948, demonstrated how the plan of the temple at Luxor was very closely related to the proportions of the human skeleton.[2]

With the arrival of Greek civilization, the temple turned itself outwards and the landscape, as Vincent Scully has described, became the place of worship.[3] At the same time, the concept of interior space was established, although only the priest was allowed to enter the temple. The mythical founders of Greek culture were rebels against the classical gods, and their temples varied according to which deities they served. This is in direct contrast with the Egyptian example, in which the building form retained remarkable uniformity over 1500 years. We have virtually no archaeological evidence about the form and structure of the small house in this era.

The period of Roman dominance coincided with a time when public buildings and large private houses became the domain of architectural expression: public and private spaces began to take on a form that we would still comprehend today. The building type that had been the temple was increasingly supplanted by structures dedicated to emperors who claimed for themselves the status of deities. Vitruvius, writing his Ten Books of Architecture in the first century BC, devotes much attention to the design of temples, public buildings and large villas, but the text is addressed to Caesar Imperator, whose 'divine intelligence and will' were otherwise engaged in 'acquiring the right to command the world'.[4]

Within the vernacular tradition, archaeological evidence dating back 5000 years suggests that the earliest form of small dwelling that could be described as a house was circular. These structures were modest, with a diameter no more than 12 metres (40 feet) and usually much smaller [Illustration 1]. They were built of timber and clay with a thatch or turf roof, or, more rarely, of stone, as at Skellig Michael in Ireland; they had central open hearths and would have housed animals as well as humans. Virtually none of the timber buildings has survived, although remarkably, as documented in Sidney Addy's The Evolution of the English House (1898), some later versions survived in Europe well into the nineteenth century.[5] He quotes the Roman writer Tacitus describing this northern European house type: '"It is sufficiently well known that none of the Germanic peoples dwell in cities, and that they do not even tolerate houses which are built in rows. They dwell apart, and at a distance from one another, according to the preference which they may have for the stream, the plain, or the grove. Every man surrounds his house with a space, either for protection against the accident of fire, or from ignorance of the art of building. They do not make use of stone cut from the quarry, or of tiles; for every kind of building they make use of unshapely wood, which falls short of beauty or attractiveness."'

The Gothic style that emerged during the Middle Ages was an artistic expression of a shared belief system. The ideas behind the great cathedrals of Europe such as Chartres were the product both of divine revelation and of the human mind. In direct contrast with the houses of the majority of the inhabitants of that period, these structures represented profound self-awareness – but it was an awareness carried in the collective will rather than in the form of individual expression. Houses, meanwhile, were still constructed according to the vernacular tradition, incorporating centuries of received wisdom. As writers such as Louis Charpentier have shown, cathedrals resulted from the activities of relatively small groups such as the Templars, who used ancient knowledge to initiate the construction of sacred spaces that were accessible to the entire population.[6] These democratic spaces were such that ordinary people could only barely sense what lay behind their form and symbolism but nevertheless understood their underlying message. In the medieval city, the differences between the cathedral and the small houses that surrounded it, in terms of capital

Illustration 1

investment, permanence and scale of structure, was extreme. Drawing on historical records, Peter Ackroyd in London The Biography describes the house of a young couple living in the city in the mid-thirteenth century:[7] 'The unfortunate pair lived in a house of wooden construction with two rooms, one above the other, and a thatched roof. In the lower room which opened onto the street there were a folding table and two chairs, with the wall "hung about with kitchen utensils, tools and weapons". Among them were a frying pan, an iron spit and eight brass pots. The upper room was reached by means of a ladder – here were a bed and mattress.' Even so, this dwelling was not that of some of the poorer residents of the city.

Outside the city, it was common at the same time in many parts of Europe for the peasants to continue to live in structures that also housed animals and stored grain. These timber-framed buildings either

had a basilica form with side aisles and a central hearth or, particularly in colder climates, took the form of long houses. Sidney Addy quotes Giraldus Cambrensis, a thirteenth-century writer describing the sleeping arrangements in one such house in Wales: '"But at last, the hour of sleep approaching, they lie down all together on a place thinly strewn with rushes and covered with hard rough cloth which the country produces and which in common parlance is called brachen. And they are clad by night as by day: for they keep off the cold at all times with only a thin and transparent cloak; they are, however, much comforted by a fire at their feet and likewise by the near heat of their sleeping companions."' The companions referred to by Cambrensis could well mean sheep, cows and pigs, reinforcing the point that our modern concept of privacy and comfort is totally different from that of the medieval period. The small rural dwelling would have meant enduring the most exposed

existence, socially, physically and economically [Illustration 2].

If we had to pinpoint a historical moment when truly self-conscious design started, it would have to be the mid-fifteenth century. This was the period when patrons began to require an architecture for their dwellings that was entirely new but rooted in the values of the past. In the first independently written and widely read architectural treatise since Vitruvius, Leon Battista Alberti argued in his On the Art of Building (1440s) that the architect's primary role was conceptual rather than practical, and that the role of good buildings was not only to function well but also to exercise a therapeutic effect on their users.[8] 'The greatest glory in the art of building is to have a good sense of what is appropriate,' wrote Alberti, clearly marking the beginnings of a new way of thinking about architecture. His ideas are recognizably modern, in that building is acknowledged to require both skill

Illustration 2

and discernment. This was precisely the point at which the house, the unique domain of the private individual, became at last a specific focus of attention for the emergent profession of artist/architect.

The dissolution of medieval society was a gradual process, so much so that the vernacular tradition in houses survived in a very pure form in Europe until the mid-nineteenth century – in England, timber-framed houses with wattle-and-daub walls and thatched roofs were still being erected by local craftsmen in 1850. If the vernacular is defined as a style of building conceived by the person who builds it, the erosion of vernacular building can be seen as directly linked to industrialization, the division of labour and the imposition on the building process of abstract artistic principles.

The mid-fifteenth century saw the emergence of a newly prosperous class, representatives of neither church nor state, who sought an architecture to reflect their growing status – it was no longer enough to rely on established building practices. This trend was made possible by a combination of early printing (allowing the dissemination of abstract ideas), a newly developed humanist philosophy, supposedly free of religious dogma, and the concentration of wealth in private hands. And yet still the small house had not recognizably entered architectural history.

Florence, the birthplace of the quattrocentro, was arguably the world's first modern state, but in 1430 it had a population of only around 50,000, and wheat fields, orchards and vineyards could still be found within the city walls. At that time, masons working under the direction of Filippo Brunelleschi on the dome of the cathedral of Santa Maria del Fiore had their wages cut to 1 lira per month as a result of a war with the nearby city state of Lucca. These workers would have lived in what we would now regard as little more than hovels only marginally larger and better built than those of the average Londoner 180 years earlier.[9] As in northern Europe, work was seasonal. If the weather was cold, laying stone or bricks in lime mortar was impossible - at such times, many would have had to resort to other trades or agricultural work.

Historians of the Renaissance have tended to focus on the achievements of the architects, artists, patrons and thinkers who brought about dramatic cultural changes in European society, but, as Lynn White has shown in Medieval Technology and Social Change, at least 90 per cent of the population were engaged in work on the land during this period, while the historical concept of civilization is essentially based on an urban perspective and relates to a tiny minority 'standing on the shoulders of the peasants'.[10] The villas of the Medicis, of Palladio, Bramante and his pupil Raphael were the exceptions: large projects for discerning clients who had huge funds available for building, and who were prepared to engage in patronage. The filtering down of high art ideas to the design of small houses for people who did not enjoy such privileges slowly began to manifest itself in a limited way. As was the case with artistic activity in general, the dissemination of consciously conceived architectural ideas was far from universal. According to Arnold Hauser in The Social History of Art, the Renaissance created an 'unbridgeable gap between an educated minority and an uneducated majority which had never been known before to this extent and which was to be such a decisive factor in the whole future development of art'.[11]

Some contemporary paintings reflect this division. Pieter Breughel's Haymaking [Illustration 3] (c.1565) shows a rural landscape peppered

Illustration 3

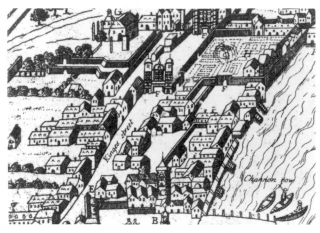

Illustration 4

Illustration 5

with clusters of vernacular buildings, but in the background, on the bank of the meandering river, lies a walled city which supports an urban-based economy that will eventually destroy the peaceful scene the painting so lovingly depicts. Breughel journeyed from his home in North Brabant to Italy in 1552; he had previously worked in the studio of Pieter Coecke, who himself had worked in Italy, and later been involved with a studio that produced prints based on paintings by Michelangelo, Raphael and Titian. Breughel's later landscape painting became a pan-European part-fantasy reflecting both a rural ideal and a cultured, civilized Renaissance architectural context – as if the works are an attempt to reconcile these two apparently opposed worlds. This is a setting in which one would not be surprised to find Cervantes's character Don Quixote, whose story was conceived in novel form and first published in 1604 as a parody of the medieval knight finding himself in a world that had long since adopted

a new set of values that make his own appear anachronistic.

Maps of cities such as Rome and London drawn in the late sixteenth century reinforce this picture. Antonio Tempesta's map of Rome of 1593 shows a city that is an amalgam of classical ruins, Renaissance public buildings and villas, and rows of anonymous town houses, some very small. Hogenberg's map of London of 1572 may show medieval fortifications encircling a network of densely packed vernacular houses, but to the west lie the riverside villas of the new merchant classes, lining the banks of the Thames up to Westminster, the seat of civil power [Illustration 4].

The rapid dissemination of the ideas generated in the relatively short period of the Renaissance was made possible by three things. First, the wealthy people of northern Europe increasingly embarked on the Grand Tour and saw for themselves

the buildings of classical antiquity. Second, printing meant that by the middle of the sixteenth century the works of both Palladio and Serlio could be examined by people outside Italy without travelling at all. And third, building skills formed part of an international labour market – for example, in England at least three Acts of Parliament were passed in the sixteenth century to protect workmen from being supplanted by skilled craftsmen brought in from mainland Europe who had experience in constructing designed, rather than vernacular, houses.

It was at the end of the sixteenth century that the first examples of small houses conceived outside the vernacular tradition began to appear in Europe. These buildings were often constructed on large country estates as little more than follies. The Triangular Lodge [Illustration 5], for example, in the English county of Northamptonshire, built in 1593 by Sir Thomas Tresham for occupation by

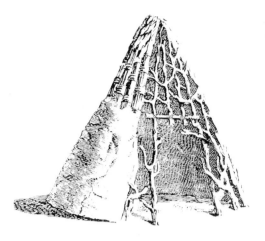

Illustration 6

Illustration 7

his gamekeeper, is neither classical nor Gothic in its stylistic treatment, but is rather a highly personal attempt to represent the concept of the Holy Trinity. The building is in plan and elevational composition consistently related to the number three and is what Tresham himself described as 'a sermon in stone'. As with Laurence Sterne's Tristram Shandy (1759), which is often referred to as the first novel, Tresham's idiosyncratic lodge breaks all the rules that its type would seem to demand. First examples of anything are often the exceptions that prove the rule.

From around 1500, at the same time as printed copies of Vitruvius started to become available, interest grew in the idea of the Ur-house, or original dwelling, seen as an idealized structure in an Eden-like garden. The link with classicism was made later, most prominently by the Abbé Laugier in his Essai sur l'architecture (1753), in which he

describes the process by which primitive man finally rejected cave dwelling:[12] 'Man wants a dwelling which will house, not bury him. Some branches broken off in the forest are material to his purpose. He chooses four of the strongest, and raises them perpendicularly to the ground, to form a square. On these four he supports four others laid across them, above these he lays some which incline to both sides, and come to a point in the middle. This kind of roof is covered with leaves thick enough to keep out both sun and rain: and now man is lodged. True, the cold and the heat will make him feel their excesses in this house, which is open on all sides; but then he will fill the in between spaces with columns and so find himself secure. This little hut which I have just described is the type on which all the magnificences of architecture are elaborated.' Laugier's original small house is nothing other than a temple made of trees in which the forms of the branches, trunks and leaves form

the basis of all the elements of classical architecture.

Other contemporary writers, including William Chambers, sought geometrical purity in the forms they imagined that Vitruvius had been describing, particularly the cone and the cube [Illustration 6]. A little later, in 1785, Sir James Hall attempted a practical demonstration with still-growing ash trees to 'prove' that Gothic had its origins in the natural forms of trees, thereby giving it a rival claim over classicism to being the origin of all true architecture. This is also the moment at which increasingly large numbers of designed projects for small houses appear. In France around 1773 Claude Nicolas Ledoux proposed a pyramid-shaped house of stacked logs designed for occupation by an estate woodcutter [Illustration 7]. In declaring the small house worthy of architectural consideration, he said:[13] 'The artist cannot always impose gigantic proportions on the eye; but

the real architect will expend the same energy on a woodcutter's house as he would on the greatest commission.'

A decade or so later Queen Marie Antoinette spurned the vast extravagances of the Palace of Versailles and based herself in the relatively small house known as Le Petit Trianon, an eight-roomed neoclassical building set in extensive grounds with its own garden; the design of the grounds was clearly influenced by the ideas of Jean Jacques Rousseau, in that it was a 'natural park' attempting to be a condensed reproduction of the landscapes experienced in different parts of the world.

In Germany the romanticized view of dwelling and landscape manifested itself from around 1829 in projects such as those in the Charlottenhof near Potsdam. There, the architect Karl Friedrich Schinkel designed a series of buildings and structures,

Illustration 8

Illustration 9

including an Italianate gardener's house and a smaller dwelling for the assistant [Illustration 8], in order to recreate in miniature the architectural experiences of Goethe's Italian journey, a trip that started in Carlsbad in 1786 and ended in Rome in 1788. The royal landscape park was intended to be not only a form of built entertainment but also a physical manifestation of the need for northern Europe to make a strong link with the cultural legacy of classical antiquity. A walk through the park, which included crossing an 'alpine' bridge, was meant to imbue an individual with the same insights that had come to Goethe himself on his travels and on which he based so much of his scientific and artistic work. This romance was in part created by the intimate scale of those buildings in contrast with the grand scale of the main palace.

In England, small lodges, gatehouses and dwellings for estate workers proliferated as the fashion for 'improvement' took hold. Pattern books with picturesque designs were readily available for patrons seeking inspiration. For example, J. Plaw's Sketches for Country Houses, Villas, etc. (1800) contains detailed drawings of numerous 'ornamental cottages'. Some architects were capable of working not only with completely different scales of building but also in different styles. John Nash – better known for his classically derived designs for the large mansions bordering London's Regent's Park – was clearly confident in producing a group of remarkably convincing pseudo-vernacular cottages for the retired servants of the banker J. S. Harford on Harford's estate near Bristol. The ten small dwellings arranged around a green each has a different design but uses a common language of materials and details [Illustration 9].

Throughout the nineteenth century there was a continuing fascination with the designs of ideal residences for country estate workers – bailiff, gamekeeper, gardener and gatekeeper. Books such as W. Audsley's Cottage, Lodge and Villa Architecture (1870) documented numerous designs in what are described as Elizabethan, Gothic or Italian style. Audsley disliked attempts to use classical elements in the design of small houses: 'While the lordly Palladian could not shrink to the humble proportions of a cottage, and the Greek appeared both out of place and ridiculous in anything of less pretensions than the temple-like hall or church, the Gothic and Elizabethan styles rejoiced alike in their innate beauty and fitness whether exhibited in the labourer's cottage, the elegant villa, or the mansion of the nobleman.'

The design and construction of such small houses was not primarily prompted by any desire to improve the living conditions of their occupants; rather, it was about the creation of a visually literate environment for landowners that expressed their status and cultural values. The period of rapid industrialization in Europe coincided with the romanticization of country life, and the reality of the poverty and harshness of life on the land was ignored in a way that still distorts our present-day view of the buildings that housed agricultural and estate workers. John Woodforde's The Truth about Cottages quotes a traveller in rural northern England describing a typical small dwelling of around 1830:[14] 'They are of one storey and generally of one room. On one side is the fireplace, with an oven on the one hand and a boiler on the other; on the opposite side of the cottage is the great partition for the beds, which are two in number, with sliding doors or curtains. The ceiling is formed by poles nailed across from one side of the roof to the other, about half a yard from where it begins to slope, and covered with matting.'

Most small rural houses of the nineteenth century that have survived to the present day were built and occupied by the relatively well off. The dwellings of the poor were not only squalid and unhealthy but also extremely ephemeral; they were either allowed to fall into ruins or were replaced by more substantially built structures [Illustration 10].

Another significant factor in the architectural development of the small house was colonization. Within three years of the landing in North America of the Mayflower, which in 1620 brought the first recorded European settlers to the continent, a local sawmill had been set up to process local timber. The houses of these pioneers in New England – one- or two-storey structures with a single room on the ground floor – were made using traditional European timber-framed construction techniques. As time passed, these houses were often enlarged, a tendency reflected in

later American houses on individual plots. In the vivid descriptions of her childhood in the 1870s, the writer Laura Ingalls Wilder recorded the rapid transformation of the lifestyles of later settlers who migrated westwards. Following their first move from Wisconsin, Laura's family settled in a one-roomed cabin built from scratch by their father using materials from the nearby prairie. Within ten years, they were living in a two-bedroomed balloon-framed house on the main street of a newly created town with a total population of around eighty people.

The balloon frame, first used in 1833, was a revolutionary system that used prefabricated elements of machine-cut timber fixed together by nails – making it highly appropriate in a country driven by the industrialization of all production processes, including agriculture and building. In his 1920 film One Week, Buster Keaton famously subverted the uniformity of these houses by following

instructions that had been tampered with and wrongly assembling the prefabricated components of his new house.

The colonization of India led to another version of the small house as a recognizable type: the bungalow. As Anthony King explains in his comprehensive historical survey, the name bungalow is derived from bangla, a house belonging to Bengal.[15] From the early nineteenth century onwards, pre-made portable houses were exported from Britain for use by the growing numbers of government officials, doctors, engineers and traders settling not only in India but in West and East Africa. The later versions had verandas, ridge ventilation and raised ventilated plinths to assist cooling [Illustration 11]. Bungalows were by definition detached and single storey, and as a typology went on to dominate suburban developments in Europe, Scandinavia and North America in

Illustration 10

Illustration 11

EAST INDIA VILLA.

the twentieth century, more often as generously sized dwellings for the middle classes than as small houses. The bungalow therefore represents a continuation of the kind of cultural interaction seen in the eighteenth-century pursuit of the Ur-house, or original dwelling. Western European culture abstracted the indigenous building forms of the newly colonized world and adapted them for its own purposes, in the same way that the quattrocento 'rediscovered' classical architecture and used its elements in an entirely new way.

All these examples lack spatial invention – a feature that came only with the advent of Modernism – but there are examples of transitional projects. One of the early works of the Scottish architect Charles Rennie Mackintosh was a series of designs for a gatehouse to be attached to the manor at Auchenbothie in Renfrewshire. The four versions for this small house all date from 1901, one year before work began on the

canonic Hill House, but remarkably Mackintosh managed to embody in all of them three essential features of the larger version: the L-shaped plan that creates a positive external space, the semicircular stair that forms a tower, and an imposing canted brick chimney that visually locks the house to the ground [Illustration 12].

At the 1851 Great Exhibition in London's Hyde Park, Prince Albert had exhibited a design for four model cottages. An urban version of this proposal, built soon afterwards in a south London park, represents an early attempt to deal with not only the aesthetics of the small house but also its occupants' health and quality of life. This was an early example of what might now be called social housing, and it was a theme taken up in other European countries. In Scandinavia, small dwellings for workers built by housing cooperatives date from around the same time. The first of these

were the rows of small architect-designed two-storey houses built in Copenhagen by the Danish Medical Association in 1853 in response to the cholera epidemic that had devastated the city earlier in the year.

The political pressure to improve housing standards transformed the basis on which small houses were built. No longer dependent on the whim of relatively rare liberal landowners, they were increasingly commissioned by collective clients such as charities, associations and large industrial concerns. These new projects reflected a new set of values, with emphasis on the internal organization of the spaces and the level of comfort they could provide. For example, from around 1900, the Cadbury company built a series of model villages for their workers in the English Midlands, using a range of designs for small dwellings – designs that incorporated some ingenious space-saving ideas and the latest available service technologies.

Illustration 12

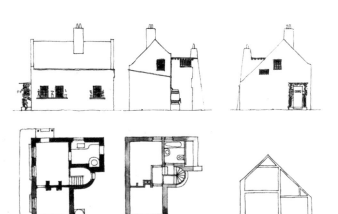

Illustration 13

One scheme had plumbed baths – still a rarity at that time – set flush into the floors of the kitchens, so that they could be covered over and take up no space when not in use[16] [Illustration 13]. But such schemes represented only a tiny percentage of housing provision.

All these projects were collectively dwarfed by the unprecedented experiment in public housing undertaken by the government of the Soviet Union after the communist revolution of 1917. Planners and architects adopted two models. The first was the garden city, as developed earlier in England, and the second was the communal house, which originated in France. An evolution of the traditional Russian 'izba' – a one-roomed timber hut, dominated by a large brick stove, that could be grouped as multiples around shared lobbies – the communal house minimized personal space and stressed the importance of shared facilities.

But politicians and designers soon realized that this model could not be forced on people, so projects for small individual houses were developed to provide what the architect Moisei Ginzburg described as 'not communal houses but a community of houses'.[17] One such project for the Magnitogorsk industrial sector envisaged partly prefabricated one-roomed houses on columns arranged in continuous ribbons providing 'a free-standing dwelling for each human being if he or she lives alone: free-standing dwellings for groups of various sizes, from one couple to any desired fraternity – surrounded by space and greenery, permeated by light and sun, freed from being squeezed into the narrow limits of the city block'.

Elsewhere, in proposals that appear visionary even today, architects such as Nikolai Ladovskii designed fully prefabricated and furnished individual cottages as part of an area that would eventually contain an extensive range of dwelling types and collectively form a 'socialist garden city' named the Green City [Illustration 14]. Only a few units were built before Stalinist reaction set in and experimentation ceased under the 'Restructuring of the Artistic Organizations' of 1932, by which all artists and designers were put under state control. Just before the end of this liberating period for artistic activity, Ladovskii's collaborator, El Lissitsky, wrote:[18] 'The Soviet architect was given the task of establishing a new standard of housing by devising a new type of housing unit, not intended for single individuals in conflict with each other as in the West, but for the masses. A good existing example of this type of housing is the log cabin, still used by the great masses of the rural population, which over the centuries has developed appropriate structural and technical construction standards. Even though these houses are the product of the handicrafts, they are in all other respects a standardized mass-production effort with each part developed and fixed in such a way that the builder can easily assemble the parts by himself. The same system was also used in the cities until industrialization produced the split between city and country.'

The urbanization of Europe as a result of the Industrial Revolution required the rapid provision of mass housing (Europe's population rose from 290 million in 1870 to 750 million in 1950, with London, as early as 1841, being the first city in the world to have more than 2 million inhabitants). As El Lissitsky noted, traditional timber buildings from the vernacular tradition had aspects to their construction that could be described as prefabrication and, under pressure to build quickly, the newly industrialized nations experimented throughout the nineteenth century with ways to prefabricate small houses.

Illustration 14

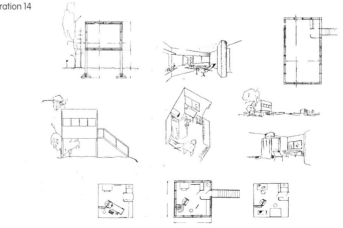

Illustration 15

Illustration 16

Probably the first prefabricated house in the industrialized world was a cast-iron tollhouse erected in 1830 on a turnpike road between Birmingham and Bromwich. Later, Richard Norman Shaw, better known for his large country houses for Victorian England's newly rich, exhibited at the 1878 Paris exhibition a small prefabricated house made of concrete panels [Illustration 15]. Acute housing shortages in the UK before the First World War (a shortfall estimated in 1918 at 600,000 units) resulted in numerous exhibitions of designs for cheap, mass-produced houses right up to the end of the First World War. A typical example was the Spieresque, a prefabricated two-bedroomed cottage shown at the Housing and Health Exhibition in Glasgow in 1919, which, it was claimed, could be erected in twenty-one days.

Germany set about dealing with its rapid urban growth at the beginning of the twentieth century by commissioning apartment blocks for the inner city and row houses for the suburbs. Bruno Taut, later prime mover in the socialist-inspired Workers for Art movement, built terraces of small two-storey houses in Berlin in 1912 that are a formalized version of vernacular cottages. Taut's visionary period, in which he instigated and took part in the exchange of architectural theories known as the Crystal Chain Letters, was followed by large housing projects in the Berlin suburbs in the 1920s. While the highly expressive forms of the dwellings drawn as part of these exchanges with his collaborators, who included Walter Gropius and Hans Scharoun, were not present in the later built works, there remained in these still-surviving suburbs a powerful sense of social purpose. In the 1930s Taut moved to Japan and lived almost as a recluse for some years in a small house that he built in the traditional style in Shorin-San. Photographed in an incongruous Western-style suit, Taut posed for the camera while sitting cross-legged on a tatami mat in a room practically devoid of furniture; in so doing, he provided us with a powerful image that connects the Modernist project with the idea of the Ur-form, or archetypal dwelling.

The strong Japanese influence is also evident in the Usonion houses of Frank Lloyd Wright. Wright first visited Japan in 1905, accompanying the Ward Willits, for whom he had designed a large house in Highlands Park, Illinois, in 1901. In typical fashion, Wright borrowed $5000 from one of his employees, Walter Burley Griffin, to make the trip, and returned with a large number of expensive Japanese prints. He returned profoundly affected by traditional Japanese domestic architecture. The first true Usonion house emerged much later, in 1936, after the lean years of the Depression. It was the result of a tentative approach by Herbert and Katherine Jacob from Wisconsin.

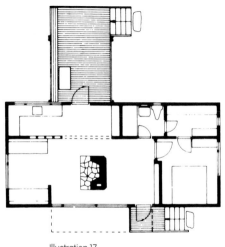

Illustration 17

The Jacobs had not expected Wright to accept the commission because they had modest funds and required a small house that could be built for $5000 including the cost of the site. But Wright was looking for a testbed for his ideas for low-cost housing incorporating features that he had already devised in theory: underfloor heating, a masonry chimney core, thin timber board and batten walls, an integrated carport instead of a garage, and a virtually flat roof without gutters or downpipes [Illustration 16]. By American standards, the house was small, at around 150 square metres (1600 square feet), with an L-plan that presented a blank, horizontally boarded façade to the road, and pavilion-like garden façades that were almost fully glazed with deep overhanging eaves.

Wright's talent for self-publicity (his private life had already been the subject of repeated public scrutiny) gained the house immediate widespread attention. The former head of the Bauhaus, Walter Gropius – who was by then, having fled Nazi Germany, lecturing at the University of Wisconsin – visited the site when the house was under construction. Wright, making a brief stop on his way to the construction site of the Johnson Wax factory, refused to meet him. Wright never liked the Bauhaus and often condemned its principles.[19]

Gropius himself had been fascinated for many years by the problem of how part-mechanization might be used to solve the problem of mass housing without producing inflexible, monotonous designs. While working in the office of Peter Behrens in 1909, he had written a proposal entitled 'A Plan for the Forming of a Company to Undertake the Construction of Dwellings with Standard Component Parts'. Although he went on to build a house for himself in Lincoln, Massachusetts, Gropius's collaboration with Marcel Breuer on a small house in Wayland of 1940 better embodies his design principles. Sigfried Giedion, in Space Time and Architecture, says the house 'hovers over the ground like a butterfly' – an effect achieved by using braced-timber balloon-frame construction to allow the raised main floor to cantilever out from a smaller rock-faced base which penetrates the living room in a reduced form as a chimney. The composition of the plan around this large solid core shows the influence of the Usonian houses [Illustration 17].

The International Congress for Modern Architecture (CIAM) met first in 1928 near Geneva and – in an attempt to support artistic freedom against what were seen as forces of reaction – drew up a manifesto for contemporary architecture. The second congress, held in Frankfurt in 1929, had as its theme Minimum Space Dwellings. Walter Gropius, Le Corbusier and Alvar Aalto all attended under the auspices of Ernest May, the head of the city's housing department. The Canadian Wells Coates – who had spent his childhood in Japan as the son of Methodist missionaries, but was by then based in London – was already working on outline designs for minimum dwellings. Coates did not attend a CIAM meeting until 1933 (which took place on a ship sailing from Marseilles to Athens, Moscow having withdrawn its offer as host) but the building of the Lawn Road Flats in north London in 1934 allowed him to combine the minimum dwelling theme with a radical social agenda [Illustration 18].

The project was the initiative of Molly and Jack Pritchard, who, together with Coates and Serge Chermayeff, had visited the Bauhaus several years previously and fully endorsed the emergent philosophy of Modernism. The Pritchards' early brief for the site, two large linked houses, was gradually replaced by a far more experimental agenda:

a five-storey block of twenty-two dwellings of effectively one room each; seven slightly larger units on each end of the block; and a large penthouse flat for the Pritchards themselves. The project was contractually radical as well. A company named Isokon was formed to act as developer, with the aim of using the Lawn Road scheme as a prototype for further projects – which, to Wells Coates's great distress, never materialized. When the flats were eventually completed, after many well-documented setbacks and high levels of stress for everyone involved, each was let at £104 per annum (£3300 in today's money) with all services included. Communal facilities included a restaurant, in-flat meals cooked by a resident chef and even a shoe-cleaning service.

Minimum living meant built-in furniture and extremely well-organized storage – features that Coates would incorporate in his most radical of small dwellings, the flat he built for himself at 18 Yeomans Row in 1935, which shows strong references to the time he spent in Japan. In the following years the Lawn Road Flats acted as a temporary refuge for people such as Walter and Isa Gropius and the artist Laszlo Moholy-Nagy, before the Pritchards sold up and moved out of London.

Charles-Edouard Jeanneret's experiments with small houses had started a little earlier. He had a 'first' career in his home town of La Chaux-de-Fonds in Switzerland, then moved to Paris in 1917 and reinvented himself as Le Corbusier. One of his many ambitions was to design mass-produced housing systems based on new technologies such as poured concrete and sandwich panels. In 1920 he began work with the painter Amédée Ozenfant on a new review called L'Esprit Nouveau, whose opening lines were: 'There is a new spirit: it is a spirit of construction and synthesis guided by clear conception … a great epoch has begun.'

In 1923 Le Corbusier published Towards a New Architecture, which set out a manifesto for his future working methodology, juxtaposing classical architecture with the products of mechanization such as aeroplanes, cars and ocean liners, in an attempt to see the temple and the machine as different aspects of the same spiritual evolution. In the same year he designed and had built a small retirement house for his parents on the shore of Lake Geneva – his mother lived there until 1960, when she died at the age of 100 [Illustration 19]. At barely 4 metres (13 feet) deep, the house is organized linearly; the main space has a window 11 metres (36 feet) long overlooking the lake. The free plan, free façade and roof garden prefigure his later iconic works such as Villa Stein (1926) and Villa Savoye (1933), but for his parents they were condensed into a total plan area of 60 square metres (650 square feet) – less space than Madame Savoye's garage at what was after all her

Illustration 18

Illustration 19

weekend retreat rather than her primary residence. When, as a young man, Le Corbusier had completed a journey around Europe taking in Greece and Turkey, he produced numerous drawings of simple vernacular houses, obviously drawn to the basic and simple lifestyles that they accommodated – a living version in his eyes of Rousseau's 'natural man'.

Towards the end of his life Le Corbusier built a cabin of 16 square metres (170 square feet) for his holiday use next to a small restaurant at Cap Martin on the French Riviera, very near the Eileen Gray house known as E-1027. The story is that he designed the cabin in forty-five minutes on 30 December 1951 while sitting in his regular eating place Rebutato; the plan was based on the Hindu symbol for rebirth (now tragically better known in its reverse form as the swastika). After his wife's death, Le Corbusier spent increasingly long periods of time

there alone, and it was from there that he took his last, fatal swim on 27 August 1965. Just before his death he had written:[20] 'We must rediscover man. We must rediscover the straight line that joins the axis of fundamental laws: biology, nature, the cosmos, a straight line unbending like the horizon of the sea.'

Bruno Taut and Le Corbusier were not alone among a generation of Modernists in seeking out towards the end of their careers small, simple living spaces. Pierre Chareau, the designer of one of the most influential houses of the twentieth century, never repeated his extraordinary experiment in the transformation of the products of industrialization into a handcrafted work of art. Following completion of the Maison de Verre in 1933, Chareau produced little work in France apart from a small weekend house for the dancer Djemil Anik in the suburbs of Paris, which in many ways seems to contradict the principles behind its

larger, more famous predecessor. Following his enforced move to the USA after fleeing German occupation, Chareau designed a rather anonymous house for himself on a site in East Hampton in the garden of the studio of the painter Robert Motherwell. Built on a tight budget from concrete blocks, the tiny cottage was almost garage-like in appearance, with a rectangular plan and a central service core containing a shower room and a kitchen [Illustration 20].

In 1937 Gerrit Rietveld exhibited a twelve-sided wooden summerhouse at the Utrecht trade fair with the intention of having the unit mass-produced. With a diameter of 7.4 metres (24¼ feet), the single-storey building had a perimeter zone of built-in bunks and service rooms, thereby leaving the central space as an open living area. Although the small prototype has little obvious visual connection with Rietveld's earlier, larger and far better known

Schroder House, the emphasis on flexibility and the radical questioning of the need for conventional bedrooms are shared themes [Illustration 21]. Comparison of this simple structure with the Dymaxion House of 1927, designed by Richard Buckminster Fuller, reveal the beginnings of a schism within the Modernist project that is still being played out today. Whereas Rietveld, like Chareau with his own house, used essentially nineteenth-century timber technology, Fuller utilized the latest lightweight materials such as duralumin and details that required precise factory assembly.

The attempt to bring architectural sensibilities to mass housing and reconnect with archetypal vernacular forms also appears strongly in the work of another participant in the second CIAM conference, Alvar Aalto. Aalto visited the USA in 1940, and on his return to Finland began work on what became known as the AA System. His concern, like

Illustration 20

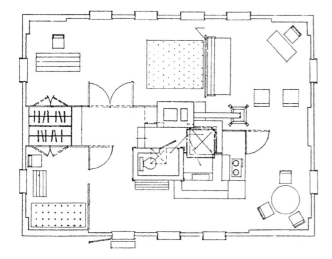

Illustration 21

Gropius's, was how to avoid monotony and lack of differentiation in the design of small houses and he sought to reflect in his designs the differences between individual circumstances. Perhaps with a touch of dry humour, he eventually proposed sixty-nine variants based on the concept of flexible standardization. Many of these variants used traditional Nordic features such as turf roofs and untreated pine-log walls. The economic and political difficulties caused by the Second World War dramatically curtailed the number of units actually built, but examples appeared in the Savonmaki and Kononpelto districts of Varkus and in Kauttua and Noormarkku [Illustration 22]. The outbuildings, particularly the sauna, at the Villa Mairea of 1937 have similar details which prefigure this work, and it is likely that Aalto was using this complex and well-funded project to experiment with ideas for his later, humbler mass-housing proposals.

Architects such as Gropius, Le Corbusier and Aalto used small houses not only to test ideas but also, more importantly, to gain major commissions for public buildings. Private houses – the bigger the better – were the primary means by which architects established their careers in the twentieth century. But the same century also saw some architects spending most of their working lives designing and building small domestic projects on tight budgets. Rudolf Schindler came to the USA from Vienna in 1914, and by 1920 was living in California and supervising construction of the Barnsdall House for Frank Lloyd Wright. Work on that project (while Wright was in Japan carrying out the Imperial Hotel commission) was not a positive experience. Aline Barnsdall never lived in the house once it was completed, and Schindler soon realized that the overbearing Wright would never allow anyone to threaten his authority, even during his absence.

Schindler's first independent design was his own home in West Hollywood, a double house that he and his wife Pauline would share with another couple. To reduce the built volume and the cost, Schindler constructed the bedrooms as open sleeping porches with canvas screens, taking advantage of the mild climate to subvert some of the most basic design assumptions. Over the next thirty years he built more than 100 houses, often acting as contractor as well as architect. Through Schindler the small house finally achieved the same architectural weight as all previous building types from villa to temple. For example, the late Armon House (1949) has an extraordinary geometry in plan and a section that allows each room to be read as part of a hierarchy of space. Its diminutive size is rendered unimportant by the complex layering of the planes of the roofs, walls, glazing and built-in furniture [Illustration 23].

Illustration 22

Illustration 23

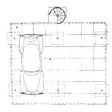

Illustration 24a

Illustration 24b

Illustration 25

The other significant figure in the evolution of the small house at that time was Albert Frey. Frey went to the USA from Zurich in 1930, having worked with Le Corbusier in Paris, where he had produced many of the construction drawings of the Villa Savoye. After forming a partnership with Lawrence Kocher, Frey designed the Aluminaire – 'A House for Contemporary Living' – for display at the 1931 Architectural League Exhibition in New York. The small steel and aluminium structure was intended to demonstrate the application of production-line techniques to low-cost housing. Its erection for the exhibition took just ten days. The house was then sold to a private buyer, Wallace Harrison, who had it re-erected on his estate on Long Island, where it was subsequently moved, crudely extended and later left to deteriorate. In 1934 Frey collaborated with Kocher to produce the even smaller and more experimental Canvas Weekend House [Illustrations 24a and 24b],

a timber-framed single volume containing one open-plan living space raised on six steel columns. Treated canvas was used as the external weather envelope and the inner linings were made of veneered plywood, thus avoiding all wet trades.

Frey's fascination with small houses continued to the end of his career. His last house, built for himself in Palm Springs in 1963, was a pure, almost fully glazed, steel-framed rectangle built around a large existing rock that acted as a divider between the sleeping and living areas. Although Frey never deviated from his early belief in lightweight construction using products of the industrial age, his houses became more and more contextual and fully integrated into the landscape.

Like Buckminster Fuller's Dymaxion and Wichita Houses, Frey's Aluminaire never went into production, but in the UK the combination of acute housing

shortages and overproduction capacity in aircraft factories after the end of the Second World War resulted in the erection of more than 150,000 small prefabricated houses. Four different types of single-storey, two-bedroomed houses were designed. The most successful was the Aluminium Temporary, a prototype of which was first exhibited behind Selfridges department store in London in the summer of 1945. The housing units were made in four sections on production lines formerly used to make fighter planes and bombers, each section being pre-finished with all its services, fitted furniture and decorations. The sections were delivered by lorry – each sized at the maximum permissible road load of 2.2 metres (7¼ feet) wide by 6.7 metres (22 feet) long - craned onto prepared concrete slabs and assembled in less than forty hours [Illustration 25].

At roughly the same time in France, the workshops of Jean Prouvé were

making prefabricated and demountable houses based on designs by Pierre Jeanneret. Prouvé used a wooden frame because of the unavailability of metal. The main feature of the house construction was a central 'wishbone' that bifurcated the plan and provided structural stability. Several examples were built as variants on the same theme, known generically as Demountable Building F 8 x 8, a name that reflected the house's modest overall dimensions. In Germany in 1958, Frei Otto erected in Berlin-Zehlendorf an atelier of about the same size that has the alternative function of a small house. The two designs both have a prefabricated structural frame, lightweight non load-bearing walls and service cores.

These projects had in common what Robert Venturi called 'industrial iconography'. Venturi's highly influential writings and built work of the 1960s and early 1970s rejected

Modernism's attempt to avoid architecture's symbolic role and argued the need to reconnect with archetypal forms:[21] 'Vitruvius wrote, via Sir Henry Wooton, that architecture was Firmness, Commodity and Delight. Gropius (or perhaps only his followers) implied… that Firmness and Commodity equal Delight; that structure plus program rather simply result in form; that beauty is a by-product; and that the process of making architecture becomes an image of architecture.'

Writing about Venturi's and Brown's Trubeck and Wislocki Houses in Nantucket (both 1971), the architectural historian Vincent Scully says:[22] 'The two new houses stand side by side on a bluff above the bay at Pocomo, with every variety of old and new shingled house, from 1973 to 1686, to be found not far away. But these two stand very much alone, and their tall vertical stance gives each of them a special quality as a person; we can empathise with them as the embodiment of sentient beings like ourselves. Indeed, Venturi has acknowledged the influence of the Greek temples at Selinus and their placement, since they turn like two bodies slightly towards each other as if in conversation. Here semiology approaches its essential, which is the action of people talking to each other: not now gods, like the being embodied, for example, in the high, taut Temple of Athena at Paestum, but common creatures dwindled to modest human scale' [Illustration 26]. In spite of his reservations about the methodology of Modernism, Venturi's insights, beautifully condensed and articulated by Scully, finally reveal a common reality to twentieth-century design practice: the house had become the new temple.

But the most prolific of American architects influenced by these post-Modern sensibilities in regard to domestic architecture is Charles Moore. Moore's work abounds with examples of spatially inventive small houses that nevertheless use traditional construction and pseudo-vernacular forms. He was a great admirer of Sir John Soane, and particularly of Soane's own house at Lincoln's Inn Fields in London, an Aladdin's cave of spatial tricks, illusions and surprises. 'There is an excitement, in my mind especially,' wrote Moore, 'of miniatures, for tiny things that carry the message of much bigger ones.'

As well as being a practitioner, Moore was, like Venturi, a teacher and academic. In his writings he stands in direct contrast to polemicists such as Wright and Le Corbusier – avoiding the manifesto, the sets of rules and the doctrines, and stressing instead symbolism, avoidance of abstraction and the importance of memory. In a series of small houses built for his own use between 1955 and 1967, Moore used Louis Kahn's ideas about servant and served spaces by either

Illustration 26

Illustration 27

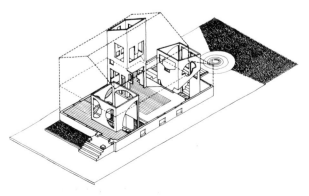

hollowing out parts of the inside of the house, or inserting even smaller structures within them, to create what he referred to as 'compressed layers'. In this way, 'a small house is seen as the centre of the universe'[23] [Illustration 27].

The transition from an overly Modernist position to the one that prevails today can be seen in the artistic development of individual architects. James Stirling's and James Gowan's Ham Common Flats of 1955 are a homage to Le Corbusier in their detailing, but the following year the duo designed a small mews house in the Kensington area of London that combines brutalist details – the sink in front of the picture window, the crude timber junctions – with a highly studied and contextual street façade in banded render that mimics its Georgian neighbours. The diminutive Kensington House contains the seeds of Stirling's development into a mannerist of the modern era [Illustration 28].

In 1966 the Danish architect Jørn Utzon, after resigning from work on the uncompleted Sydney Opera House, returned to his studio in Hellbaek and began work on the Espansiva system of housing. As a young man, Utzon had travelled to China and Japan, and throughout his working life drew heavily on his copy of the first-ever printed architectural treatise, the Ying tsao fa shih, from the Chinese Song Dynasty. The treatise systematically set out a range of building elements that are capable, in different permutations, of forming all types of building, from small house to temple. Utzon used this as the basis for what he described as 'additive architecture':[24] 'By studying the history of the one family house right up to the present day we find that our requirements can best be met by a house on posts or columns where the roof and floor form solid, uninterrupted slabs whilst the non-bearing outer walls and the inner walls between the columns are flexible. We have therefore divided the column house into modules or units of size, which correspond to the different functions of the rooms, and we have a completely free choice in composing our houses from these modules.'

Utzon planned variants that ranged in size from one-roomed huts to three-bedroomed houses, but only one prototype was built, in Gammel Hellebaek north of Copenhagen [Illustration 29]. Utzon - who along with Philip Johnson is the last surviving member of the heroic age of Modernism - used his intuition and ability to observe the world in such a way as to avoid both the reductivism of a vision in awe of the machine and an eclecticism that views all value systems as equal in value.

The small house entered architectural history, in the form of a consciously designed artifact, as a kind of eccentricity. It later evolved into an extension of the aesthetics of power statements by the rich. An increasing sense of individualism brought a corresponding sense of moral responsibility, and patronage began to be concerned with the social dimension of architecture. Modernism, the Rubicon of the First World War (the first mechanized war) and the expansion of the individual artistic impulse into all realms of life finally allowed the small house to embody all aspects of architecture's role in human evolution.

The economic and technological developments that transformed the cultural implications of the term 'small' only really took hold after the Second World War, and the past fifty years have seen a steady trend towards miniaturization. In the 1960s it was manifested in fashion and automobile design – the mini skirt and the Mini car. Since then, many consumer durables have reinforced the trend, most obviously phones, cameras, computers and electronic equipment. No longer synonymous with lack of privilege, small houses

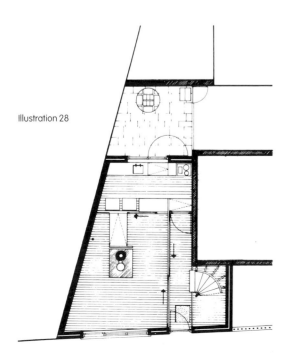

Illustration 28

Illustration 29

symbolize a range of values: compactness, efficiency, discreteness, discrimination, minimalism – as distinct from the architecture of the past, where scale was inevitably in proportion to importance and power.

The trend is driven by social realities. According to United Nations statistics, the average number of occupants per dwelling in Europe at present is 2.2 and falling. A recent survey revealed that less than 40 per cent of houses in the UK are lived in by nuclear families, and 35 per cent are occupied by people living alone; the picture is similar in other post-industrial nations.[25] In the world's major capitals, even the super-rich can no longer afford large amounts of living space for their exclusive use.

In the future, given the correct artistic insights and progressive social forms, the small house will play an increasingly important role in helping to develop our individual and collective humanity, each unit potentially expressing both what makes human beings unique and what makes us socially cohesive. No longer confined to the realm of privilege, architecture may at last become truly democratic and accessible to everyone.

' The cleverer I am at miniaturizing the world, the better I possess it. But in doing this, it must be understood that values become condensed and enriched in miniature. Platonic dialectics of large and small do not suffice for us to become cognizant of the dynamic virtues of miniature thinking. One must go beyond logic in order to experience what is large in what is small.'

Gaston Bachelard, 1958

Notes

1   On Adam's House in Paradise
    by Joseph Rykwert
    Museum of Modern Art 1972

2   The Temple in Man
    by R.A. Schwaller de Lubicz
    Inner Traditions International 1981

3   The Earth, the Temple
    and the Gods
    by Vincent Scully
    Yale University Press 1962

4   The Ten Books of Architecture
    by Vitruvius
    Dover 1949

5   The Evolution of
    the English House
    by S.O. Addy
    George Allen and Unwin 1898

6   The Mysteries
    of Chatres Cathedral
    by Louis Charpentier
    Rilko Books 1972

7   London The Biography
    by Peter Ackroyd
    Chatto and Windus 2000

8   Leon Battista Alberti –
    Master Builder of
    the Italian Renaissance
    by Antony Grafton
    Hill and Wang 2000

9   Brunelleschi's Dome
    by Ross King
    Pimlico 2000

10 Medieval Technology
    and Social Change
    by Lynn White
    Oxford University Press 1962

11 The Social History of Art Vol 2
    by Arnold Hauser
    Routledge Kegan Paul 1951

12 On Adam's House in Paradise
    by Joseph Rykwert
    Museum of Modern Art 1972

13 Visionary Architects
    Exhibition Catalogue of the University of St
    Thomas, Houston USA 1968

14 The Truth about Cottages
    by John Woodforde
    RKP 1969

15 The Bungalow
    by Anthony King
    RKP 1984

16 Bournville – Model Village
    to Garden Suburb
    by Michael Harrison
    Phillimore 1999

17 Quoted in Russian Housing
    in the Modern Age
    by William Craft Brumfield
    and Blair Ruble
    Cambridge University Press 1993

18 Quoted in Russia,
    an Architecture for
    World Revolution
    by El Lissitsky
    Lund Humphries 1970

19 Reported in Many Masks
    by Brendan Gill
    Putnams 1987

20 Quoted in Le Corbusier
    and the Continual Revolution
    in Architecture
    by Charles Jencks
    Moncelli 2000

21 Learning from Las Vegas
    by Robert Venturi, Denise Scott Brown
    and Steven Izenour
    MIT Press 1977

22 The Shingle Style Today
    by Vincent Scully
    George Braziller 1974

23 Quoted in L'Architecture D'Aujourd'hui
    March/April 1976

24 Quoted in Jørn Utzon. The Sydney Opera House
    by Françoise Fromonot
    Electra 1998

25 Figures taken from Home Alone
    The Housing Research Foundation, 1998

Chapter 01
Rural Retreats

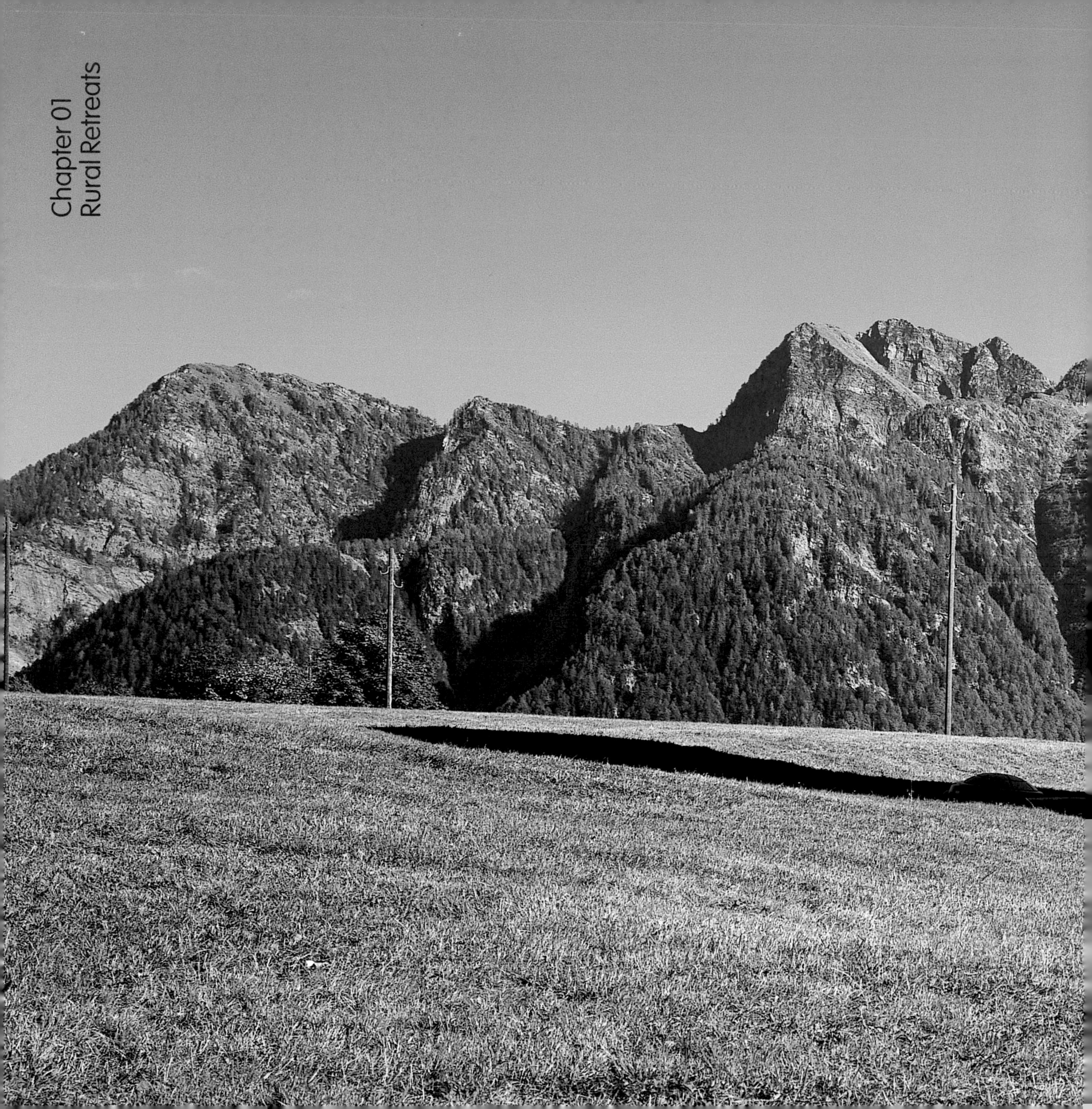

Hall on Syros
Greece 1995
Walter Pichler
100m² (1080 sq ft)

Syros is one of the smaller islands of the Cyclades and, in spite of its relative proximity to the mainland and its air link to Athens, has managed to resist the worst excesses of tourism. But the island has a number of part-time residents who are not Greek, including the German owners of this one-roomed hall designed by the Austrian artist Walter Pichler.

Pichler had previously said he would not undertake building design work outside his own farm complex at St Martin an der Raab in Burgenland, where, since 1972, he has carried out a series of restorations and new buildings to house his own sculptures. The buildings at St Martin often predate the sculptures, which are never sold but are occasionally moved out for exhibition elsewhere. Pichler finances his work through the sale of his drawings, which means

that the sculptures themselves, and the buildings that house them, can evolve over long periods with no deadline for completion.

Michael and Katerina Wurthle first invited Pichler to Syros in 1990, and from that time onwards he was involved in a project to build a 'house for stones' on one of the terraces below a converted stable, which the Wurthles live in for half the year. Apart from the fact that Michael has a very strong affinity with building and working in stone, he and Pichler are friends and had previously built a boat together. Peter Pilz, who had worked on the St Martin buildings, also provided practical help on the Syros project.

The final dimensions of the hall were suggested by the site. The abundance of local stone and Pilz's passion for the material meant that

Right
The stone hoist mechanism.

Far right
Drawing of the sculptural washing facilities.

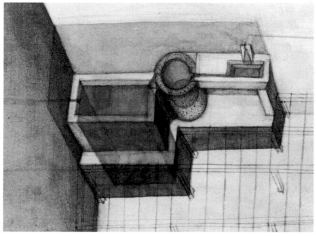

Right
The main façade is based on the indigenous architecture of the island.

the basic shell was made of loadbearing masonry. Pichler says that the original plan for the hall dissolved and turned into something else but it was never the intention to create architecture. The form and detail suggest a combination of temple form and work hall - the sacred and the profane. Pichler's research included studying and making detailed drawings of anonymous buildings on the island, measuring roof angles and eaves details, in an attempt to eliminate any sense of interpretation.

Overtly architectonic elements have been reduced to a crane installation and a raised platform with water trough inside the hall. The crane is the engine that animates the house; its symbolic function is far more important than its practical function to move large blocks of stone. Traditional Greek houses in the Cyclades often have raised platforms at one end, and the space underneath is traditionally used for storing wine and olives. In the hall Pichler has transformed this feature by creating a sculptural installation from found pieces to suggest both a shrine and a kitchen/dining space on a slightly higher level than the work space; there is no bathroom. This might not seem to be a small house in present-day terms, but by reinvesting domestic space with a sense of ritual Pichler has returned the small house almost to its point of origin, or Ur-form, charged with artistic significance and potential.

Above
Terraces lock the built form into the landscape.

Right
Using the simplest of elements Pichler has reinvested the domestic routine with the possibility of ritual.

Atelier House

Lüen, Switzerland 1996
Dieter Jüngling and
Andrecs Hagmann
62m² (670 sq ft)

Above
The house replaces
an earlier outbuilding.

In Johanna Spyri's novel Heidi, first published in 1880, a young girl's life with her grandfather in an Alpine mountain cottage is contrasted with her subsequent enforced stay in urban Frankfurt, where she can see 'nothing but stony streets'. Heidi's reclusive grandfather, Uncle Alp, is a version of the noble savage, living a life apparently untouched by industrialization, devoid of the complexities of relationships, and informed only by the rhythms of nature. On first entering the small house, Heidi is confronted by 'a biggish room which was the whole extent of his living quarters. She saw a table and a chair, and his bed over in one corner. Opposite that was a stove, over which a big pot was hanging. There was a door in one wall which the old man opened, and she saw it was a large cupboard with his clothes hanging in it. One held his shirts, socks and handkerchiefs, another plates, cups and glasses, while on the top one were a round loaf, some smoked meat and some cheese. Here, in fact, were all the old man's possessions.'

The idea of the primitive hut remote from the everyday world has continued to attract people disenchanted with urban living. Among them were two architectural photographers, one from Stuttgart and one from the Swiss region of Ober Engadin, who decided to move to a hamlet in the mountains, fifteen minutes' drive from Chur, along a small winding road. The compact collection of buildings was made up mostly of 'Strickbauten', 'knitted' buildings made of logs half jointed at the corners. The local planning restrictions prohibited any new

Top
Timber cladding reflects the appearance of traditional log construction.

Above
The junction of the new and old.

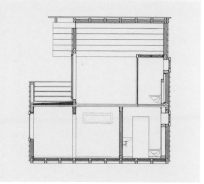

Top
Cross-section and long section.

Above
Ground- and first-floor plans.

building in the hamlet, but a small studio house was allowed on condition that it was exactly the same size and shape as the stable that it would replace on the site. The little house is directly next door to another dwelling. There is a photographic studio on the ground floor, and above that is a self-contained one-roomed apartment with its own terrace overlooking the hillside and the mountains beyond. The completed project exemplifies not only how to create a minimal space for living and working but also how to reinterpret a vernacular aesthetic without losing the integrity of the original.

The earlier log construction has been replaced by a timber frame with cladding which uses planks that retain the radial form of tree trunks. The planks are separated by small-section timber battens that give the façade a strong horizontal banding. Timber-framed windows are set flush with the outer surface and given wide surrounds to resemble cutouts. The internal lining is in sheets of birch or MDF (medium-density fibreboard), with sheet glass being used instead of tiling in the bathrooms.

In the fictional account, it takes Heidi two hours, plus a long midday rest, to walk from her home town to her grandfather's mountain cottage, reinforcing the sense of physical isolation. In rural retreats of the twenty-first century, the presence of cars, piped services and electronic communications means that remote places no longer define the minutiae of life but rather act as picturesque backdrops to activities historically associated with the city.

Right
The external stair leads to the one-roomed apartment on the first floor.

Top left and right
Shower room and
kitchen are accessed
via sliding screens.

Above
The view from the
photographer's studio.

Left
Finishes avoid
wet trades.

Casa Campo Vallemaggio

Italy 2000
Roberto Briccola
76m² (820 sq ft)

The point of departure for this little weekend house is the aesthetic of the traditional Alpine granaries of the Walser valley. More than seventy-five years ago Le Corbusier included an illustration of a grain silo in his manifesto *Towards a New Architecture* and in doing so proposed a positive role for industrialization in human artistic development: 'A great epoch has begun. Industry, overwhelming us like a flood which rolls on towards its destined end, has furnished us with new tools adapted to this epoch, animated by the new spirit.'

Like Bruno Taut, Le Corbusier had read as a young man the nineteenth-century German philosopher Friedrich Nietzsche, and had been profoundly influenced by his theory of nature as given reality and thought as created reality. This philosophy evolved into the idea that human beings should strive to attain higher forms of existence - which is not the same as working against what exists. Hence, in architecture, buildings should represent a higher form of nature rather than stand in opposition to it. Le Corbusier refined this idea, but his work, with its insistence on piloti, often implied that separation from the earth was a necessary aspect of the new architecture. The monastery of La Tourette (1953–77) and the Unité blocks (1947–52), both relatively late works, both exhibit this characteristic.

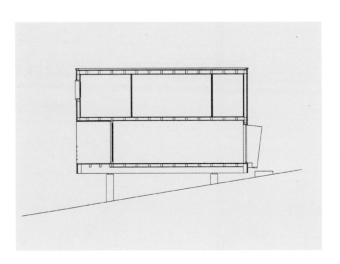

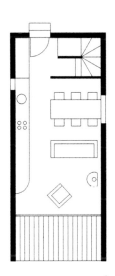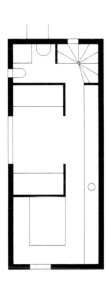

Above left
Section: the house is raised on piloti above the alpine meadow.

Above
Foundation level, ground-floor and first-floor plans; within the compact envelope are a living space, a loggia, two bedrooms and a shower room.

Above
The siting of the
house allows for
future extension.

Left
Apart from the
concrete piloti, the
house is constructed
entirely in timber.

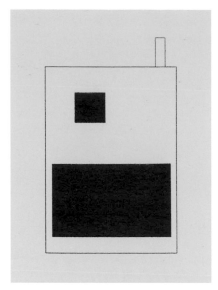

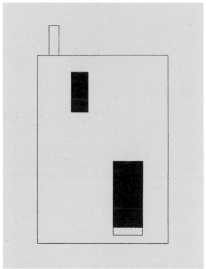

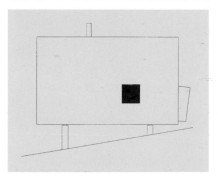

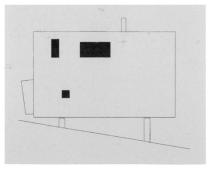

Casa Campo sits on four concrete piles, so that the compact mass of the house appears to hover over the untouched landscape. Its tenuous connection with the ground is emphasized by the welded-steel entrance porch that cantilevers out from the body of the house like a miniature aircraft loading dock. The accommodation is contained within a rectangular timber box with a plan area of 4 x 9.5 metres (13 x 31 feet). On the ground floor, the view of the mountains is framed by an integral south-facing loggia that forms an extension to the living room. The zoned kitchen top extends practically the entire length of the west wall of this room, visually exaggerating the tunnel-like portions of the space. On the first floor are two sleeping areas and a shower room linked by a passage containing another linear element, a bank of storage units with full-height sliding doors.

The abstract geometrical qualities of this small house are most evident in the façades. Windows are either squares or rectangles formed of approximate double squares - the same ratios are used in horizontal or vertical configurations and at different scales; their proportions are emphasized by linings that project externally beyond the surface of the horizontal larch boarding that forms the cladding.

Internal linings are made from laminated sheeting, which is detailed without cover strips, skirtings or architraves so that it can be read as a series of planes. Seen through the deep window apertures punctured in these simple surfaces, the landscape takes on an additional intensity. The landscape, in this vision, becomes a backdrop to refined activity, allowing a near-solitary contemplation of the forces of nature from a space that is conceptually as far removed from it as possible.

Left
Minimalist detailing in
the interior puts nature
into stark contrast.

Ching Cabin

Maury Island,
Washington, USA 1997
Miller I Hull Partnership
60m² (650 sq ft)

Above
The house seen from
the southwest across
one of the two ponds
in the grounds.

Right
The form is influenced
by the anonymous
local vernacular.

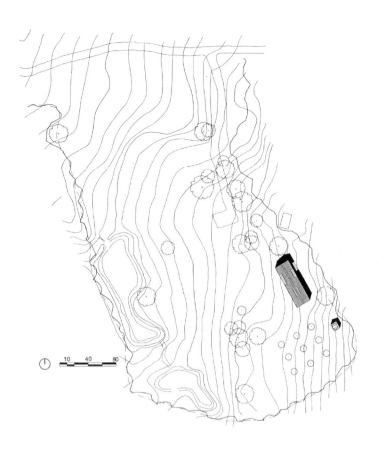

The design of Ching Cabin was influenced not only by the vernacular buildings of Maury Island, Washington State, but also by the simple but intricately detailed forms of traditional Japanese dwellings. Since the 1870s, North America has maintained an interest in its own early colonial architecture. The search for roots, for a physical manifestation of a purer and less complex life, can be seen in vacation houses and cabins across the continent, where the American dream can be played out – at weekends at least. But most of these houses could not be described as small. According to the latest United Nations statistics, the average size of a dwelling in the USA is 187 square metres (2012 square feet), twice that in any European nation, and three times the size of average dwellings in former Eastern Bloc countries. At around 120 square metres (1290 square feet) each, neither Mies van der Rohe's iconic weekend retreat for Dr Farnsworth at Plano, Illinois (1940) nor Philip Johnson's Glass House in Cambridge, Massachusetts (1942) for his own use can be described as small in this context.

However, at a mere 60 square metres (650 square feet) for a family of four, the Ching Cabin is a more convincing example of a weekend retreat, set in a gently sloping meadow that includes an orchard and two ponds, surrounded by dense woods of madrona and alder trees. The cabin is located unobtrusively on the eastern boundary of the site. Under a metal-clad gable roof are three linked elements, the living accommodation, a covered outdoor area and a tractor shed, while to the south is an elliptically shaped pump house for the water well.

Above
Site plan.

Right
Cross-section
and long section.

Below right
Plan. The sleeping
platforms are at each
end of the living space.

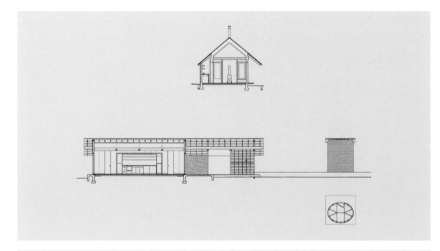

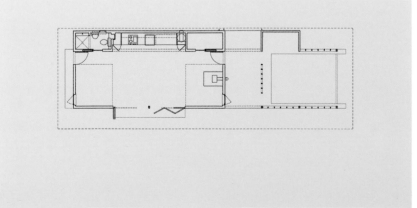

Top
Southwest-facing
veranda with
polycarbonate
rainscreen.

Above
The timber frame
construction is
fully revealed in
the tractor shed.

Right
Exploded isometric
of the main
constructional
elements.

The living space has a strong axis of symmetry, on either side of which the main components of the plan balance each other – at each end of the space is a sleeping platform, and a service zone along the back wall comprises a centrally placed kitchen flanked by a shower room on one side and a built-in cupboard on the other. Opposite the kitchen, large southwest-facing doors open onto a timber deck that overlooks the meadow, orchard and ponds. The formally elegant plan is generated by a structural timber frame built off a raised concrete slab. The frame is most visible at the tractor-shed end of the building, with its open horizontal cladding, making strong visual references to Japanese pavilions with their careful delineation of surface and space.

The cladding is cedar boarding, while the metal roof is supported on timber sheathing on exposed rafters, cut down at the eaves to give the roof a sense of lightness. Polycarbonate panels are let into the roof to form roof lights over the kitchen and the tractor shed, while over the veranda a similar detail provides a rainscreen without reducing the daylight in the living room.

In contrast with early colonial houses, which were clearly built to protect their inhabitants against the harsh climate, with its extremes of heat and cold, this house does not suggest a series of impenetrable walls, but rather in the Japanese tradition a sense of openness to its external surroundings. This is architecture that represents not a gesture of defiance but that most difficult concept for the Western mind: active passivity.

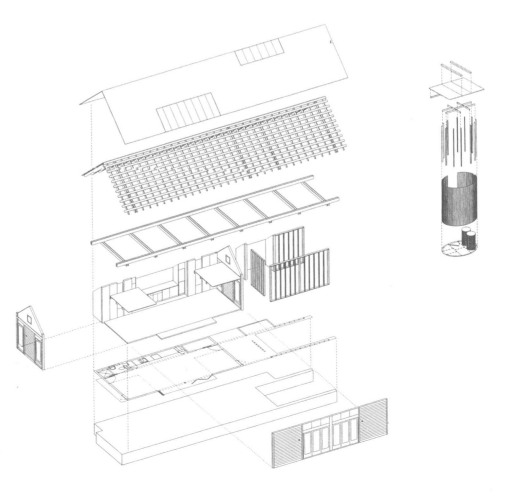

Right
The structural frame
and axial planning
define the interior space.

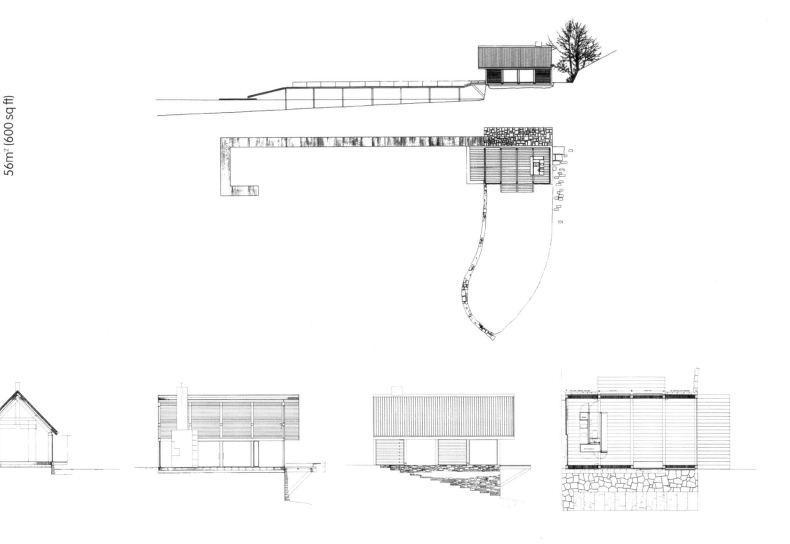

Top
Site section
and site plan.

Above
Cross section,
long section, north
elevation and plan.

Set on the banks of an inland estuary in southwest Cork, the Think Tank Boathouse is an autonomous unit within the grounds of a larger period house. Located at the bottom of a hill, it not only provides a mooring for boats but also – in the rapidly changing weather conditions of southern Ireland – offers a sheltered space from which to view the dramatic wetland landscape. The sky, the quality of the light and the ubiquitous water are the dominant features, but these are only part of a broader scene that includes the other boathouses lining the riverbank – stone and slate vernacular buildings with few or no window openings.

These simple but elegant structures with their steeply pitched roofs have clear visual connections with the archetypal forms that the Italian architect Aldo Rossi sought to reveal in his work. From Rossi's work came the paradox of a new vernacular that carries the full weight of architectural history, embodied in forms that 'being autonomous, may also be available for successive transformations'. Such forms provide both physical and symbolic protection and, according to Gumuchdjian, direct and encourage certain positive feelings in us.

The Think Tank Boathouse appears from a distance to be little different from its neighbours – a long house clad in cedar and set on a stone plinth with one axis of symmetry. Closer inspection reveals a more complex structure with subtle asymmetries and cladding incorporating fully glazed panels with or without cedar louvres. Seen from the approach path to the east, the boathouse has a jetty to the north and an artificially created pond to the south which, in contrast to the heavily tidal river, has a constant level of water. People entering the house from the land side must negotiate a large, steel-framed, sliding entrance door. When inside, they are

Top
The Think Tank
sits on the banks
of a tidal estuary.

Far left
The artificially
created pond
on the south side.

Left
The approach
path down from
the main house.

immediately treated to a stage-managed view of the opposite bank of the river, seen from off-centre of the single-volume space.

Conceived as a large piece of furniture, a service core in the first bay of the four-bay structure contains a small kitchen, a shower room/lavatory and a large storage unit for books and equipment. The structural frame of iroko hardwood is clearly visible internally with its trussed rafters and solid eaves beams. The exceptionally high wind loadings meant that the columns had to be made of steel I-sections clad in iroko, but otherwise the frame has been made by local joiners in the traditional manner. Other elements of the envelope are more specialized – the stainless-steel framing elements for the glazing had to be prefabricated elsewhere because of the lack of local skills in working this material. The Danish bleached-pine flooring system conceals underfloor heating. The fully glazed west wall overlooking the estuary comprises double-glazed units with no glazing bars but simply vertical silicon joints – a detail that produces dramatic visual effects when the rain hits the glass horizontally, as it often does in winter. In a one-off structure such as this, the mixing of vernacular and invented details is expensive, but Philip Gumuchdjan sees the building as a prototype to test ideas with far wider application.

Top
View south down
the estuary.

Above
At night the delicacy
of the building is
more apparent.

Top
Seen from the jetty.

Above
Natural and created
forms co-exist in
dramatic juxtaposition.

Above and right
The building is
an observatory
for the constantly
changing clouds,
light, and water.

Above
The west-facing gable
wall is fully glazed.

Above
The iroko frame is
designed to withstand
high wind loadings.

Above
The interior relies
on sophisticated
technology to
protect it from the
harsh external
environment.

D'Alessandro
House

São Paulo, Brazil 1998
Vinicius Andrade and
Marcelo Morettin
62m² (670 sq ft)

This house embodies in a clear but modest way the three irreducible organizing principles of any architecture: hierarchy, geometry and conformity to an established typology. The inspiration in this case was the juxtaposition of two volumes, one heavy and closed, the other light and transparent – an arrangement that produces two contrasting orders of space that conform to Louis Kahn's principle of the servant and the served. The servant is the concrete and brick service core containing a kitchen, utility space and shower room. The served is a single living space measuring 9.4 x 4 x 3 metres (30 x 13 x 10 feet), constructed with a slender timber frame enclosed primarily with polycarbonate panels. This space is built off three brick sleeper walls that visually detach it from the ground – an effect exaggerated by the cantilever of the floor deck at each end. The supporting sleeper walls appear to grow out of the core, which is itself conventionally built on footings that anchor the entire building in the ground.

Although built for use by a couple, the house has its typological origins in the Brazilian longhouses called boii – much larger structures that could accommodate up to 100 permanent residents. Inhabitants of these houses, which were first recorded by sixteenth-century travellers, slept in cotton hammocks strung between timber posts and cooked on open fires set into the earth floors. There were no dividing walls in these linear spaces, but the organization of the living areas was hierarchical. Such buildings were ephemeral; they were often rebuilt every four to five years – roughly the lifespan of the pindo palm covering the roofs. Later versions of the longhouse had internal subdivisions for individual families, and contemporary illustrations show them surrounded by timber palisades for defence.

Below
Concept drawings
showing the duality
of heavy and
lightweight elements.

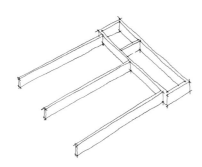
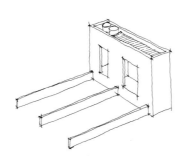

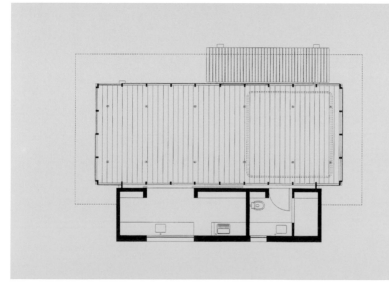

Top left
The house sits in a small
area of woodland
adjacent to a lake.

Top right
Polycarbonate panels
form the envelope of
the living space.

Above left and right
Side views show
the service core
and supporting
sleeper walls.

Left
Plan employs
Louis Kahn's
concept of servant
and served spaces.

Above
At night the interior
is back-projected
onto the screen walls.

The main hall or living space in
the D'Alessandro House is simply
organized with no formal divisions.
The sleeping area at one end is
closed off by drawing a ceiling-
mounted curtain; there is an area in
the middle for working, and an area
for relaxing and looking at the view of
the nearby lake from the only corner
of the room with clear glazing. The

polycarbonate sheet, the slender
timber columns and the thinness of
the roof (articulated and detailed as a
separate shallow-pitched metal rain
screen above the horizontal plane
of the room envelope), all suggest
transience and interest in light rather
than matter. In the core, this theme is
reversed in terms of construction and
fittings – the kitchen and bathroom
surfaces are in cast concrete.

The site, on the outskirts of São Paulo,
is a small area of woodland sloping
down to a lake. The position of the
house was dictated by the dense
tree cover, which was retained to
provide shade. If the house ever fell
into ruin, only its core would remain,
appearing as an outcrop of rock in
the landscape.

Top
The sundeck with
a view of the lake.

Above
View of the living space
from the kitchen.

Top
Only at the corner
of the living room
is there clear glass.

Above
The sleeping area
can be curtained
off for privacy.

Kawanishi Camping Cottage

Nigata, Japan 1998
Atelier Bow-Wow
64m² (690 sq ft)

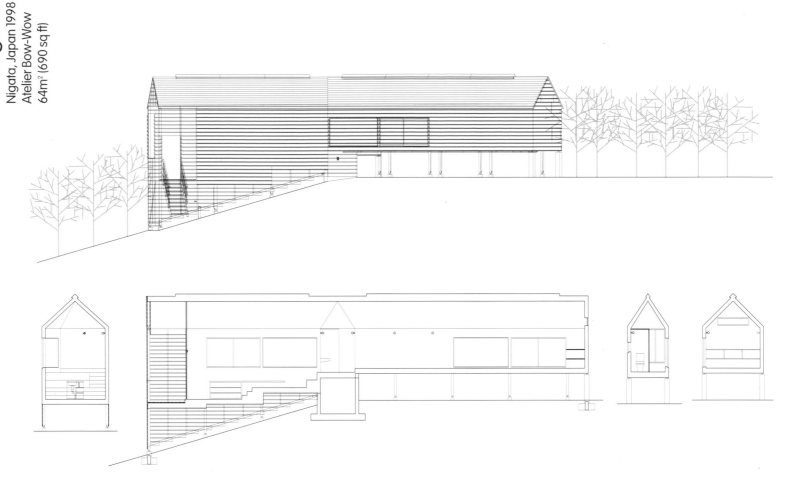

Top
East elevation.

Above
Cross-sections through the house showing the different widths of the radial wings.

Right
Site plan.

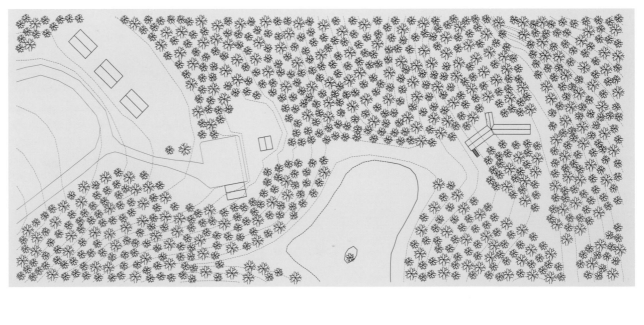

The origins of the 'butterfly plan' are obscure, but by the end of the nineteenth century there were large country house examples in England including Home Place in Norfolk by Edward Prior and Papillon Court in Leicestershire by Edwin Lutyens. Herman Muthesius, author of Das englische Haus, returned from his studies in England and produced designs of his own based on the same organizing principles, such as the house for Hermann Freudenberg in Berlin (1907). Examples by architects such as Bruce Price can also be found in the USA.

Indeed, by the beginning of the twentieth century, the authority of the right angle as a basic plan generator was being regularly questioned. The Amsterdam School, responsible for influencing the design of much mass housing in Amsterdam at that time, used versions of the butterfly plan to create a spatial dynamic, as in Michel de Klerk's housing at Spaarndammerlantsoen (1917). At the same time in Russia, the constructivist architect Nikolai Ladovskii produced experimental communal housing blocks with radial arms connected to a central core – a development of the earlier idea. A late International Style house, which has three wings with subtle differences in scale and fenestration, is Amyas Connell's 'High and Over' in Amersham, England. All these examples exploit the possibilities of the butterfly plan for multidirectional views and compact circulation.

The Kawanishi Camping Cottage has an asymmetric radial-arm plan in which each wing is a different size and each floor is set at a different level. The upper ground floor is for sleeping accommodation, while the short wing at the intermediate level is for washing and bathing. The kitchen wing steps down in sympathy with

Top
Entrance stair
leading to balcony.

Above
In winter, the house is
partially buried in snow.

the terrain below and is terminated by an entrance deck that also serves as a balcony. The building is flanked by deciduous trees in a clearing on the crest of a hill above a lake – already a natural camping place .

Located in the prefecture of Niigata, by the coast northwest of Tokyo, the cottage is the first in a series of projects designed to provide overnight shelter in a forest popular as a camping and recreation centre. In winter, snow can reach a depth of 4 metres (13 feet) - hence the decision to raise the house on timber stilts and adopt a series of narrow sections capped by steeply pitched roofs. In fact, each of the wings has a different width, so a common ridge line results in slightly varying pitches that all meet at the central point.

The area experiences periodic earthquakes, a potential problem for narrow-section buildings on stilts, but the plan gives the cottage lateral stability, with the three wings acting together when dynamically loaded. The structure is timber-framed with external horizontal boarding that acts as a rainscreen and internal ply sheet stained black to highlight the views out. The windows are shuttered and staggered on either side of external walls in each wing – a device that gives multiple and complex views of the trees and lake. The walls are otherwise kept free of clutter. The kitchen is a single linear island unit that also serves as a fixed dining table for up to eight people. Apart from the washing area, there are no rooms as such in the cottage; the interior is a continuous space divided up only by the floor levels and the directional wings.

Above
Constructional sections. Left to right: bathroom, sleeping area, kitchen.

Below
Plan.

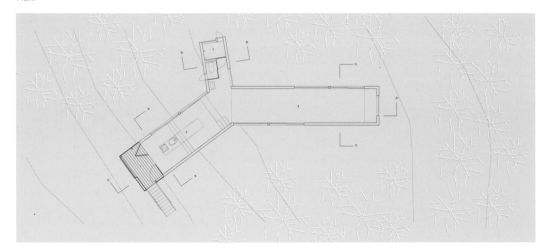

Opposite page
View of kitchen and dining space from the sleeping area.

Casa Les Meranges

Catalonia, Spain 1999
Álvarez and Minguillón
110m² (1200 sq ft)

Right
With its shutters closed,
the house resembles
an agricultural building.

The primary inspiration for this house in the Catalan Pyrenees came from the agricultural buildings of the surrounding countryside of Cerdanya. Used for storing dried straw, these structures have monolithic walls with a timber façade to the south to assist the drying of animal feed. They are normally long and shallow, built along the escarpments of the mountainous landscape. Each is covered with a monopitch roof of tiles or profiled metal, part of which is often extended to form a covered external area.

Such a combination of simple forms and materials can be found throughout northern Spain, Italy, the Balkans and Greece, and has been the basis of a number of reinterpretations by influential twentieth-century architects. For example, Le Corbusier's holiday hut at St Martins of 1950 is based on such a model, as are Jørn Utzon's Fredensborg houses of 1959, later to be elaborated into his seminal work Canne Felix on the Spanish island of Majorca. A common theme in these works is the attempt to subvert visual references to the building as a house while preferring an aesthetic that implies a workshop or a sophisticated shed. Indeed it is one of the paradoxes of the Modern movement that, while architects increasingly focused their attention on the domestic environment in the twentieth century, they themselves have generally wished to live in anything other than houses.

Below
Within the village context, the house appears unremarkable.

Below
Site plan at ground and first-floor levels.

Below
The large porch visually expands the otherwise narrow form of the house.

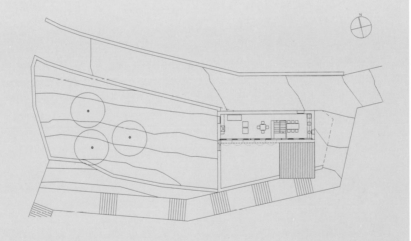

Álvarez and Minguillón designed this house in such a way that when its timber shutters are closed it resembles the surrounding agricultural buildings and reveals nothing of its true function. Since the house is only 4 metres (13 feet) deep, all the major windows are set within the south-facing timber wall so that the closed shutters merge seamlessly with its vertically boarded surface. Those few windows that are positioned within the stone walls are small and square, mere punctures in the masonry.

The main living space is on the first floor, set under the exposed roof timbers and separated from the kitchen by the open stair. At ground level there are two bedrooms, service rooms and a hall that doubles as a store room and a laundry. This arrangement is a deliberate inversion of the bourgeois convention by which rooms where work takes place are hidden from sight. The porch adjoining this hall is supported on a free-standing stone wall that has a large cutout to frame the views of the buildings below. This wall is itself a vertical extension of the retaining wall to the terrace, so that it appears fully integrated into the overall form and visually locked into the landscape.

Planning laws meant that local stone had to be used externally, but the stone is faced onto an inner core of brick, which is left unplastered internally and merely painted. The interior fittings are minimal and unsophisticated, in keeping with the idea that this is a barn that combines the environmental comforts of a house and the scenery of a chateau.

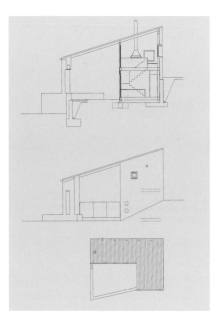

Above
Section, east elevation
and roof plan.

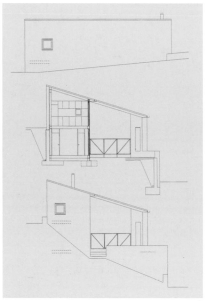

Above
North elevation,
section through porch,
west elevation.

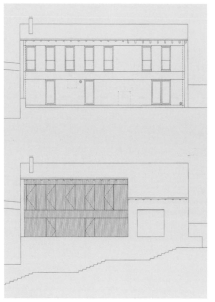

Above
Long section and
south elevation.

Above
The enclosing walls are
of local stone and have
small window openings.

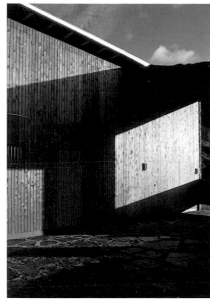

Left
Façade with
shutters open.

Below
Façade with
shutters closed.

Above
Details of the south-
facing timber façade.

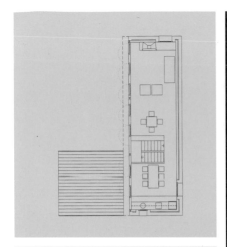

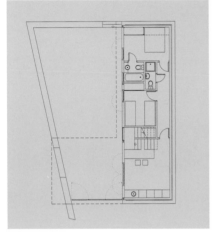

Above
First-floor plan and
ground-floor plan.

Right
View from first floor.

Left and below
The first-floor living
space is 4m (13 ft) wide
and runs the entire
length of the house.

Little House, Vilches

Talca, Chile 1995
Smiljan Radic
22m² (240 sq ft)

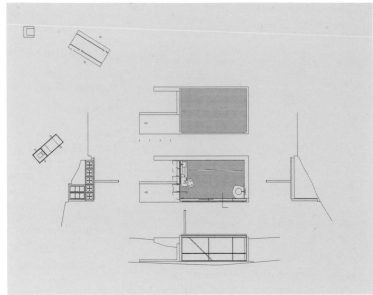

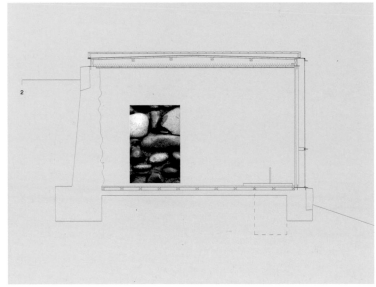

Top
Plan at roof and
ground level with
principal elevations.

Above
Section.

Abbé Laugier's idealized version of the primitive hut (1753) established this type of framed structure as the Ur-form that grew out of the human rejection of cave dwelling. The pavilion and the cave are at opposite poles in terms of architectural typologies; for the phenomenologist Gaston Bachelard, they can co-exist in the ideal house but are transformed into the garret and the cellar. In the garret we have clear rational thoughts informed by light and air, while in the cellar we become irrational and are subject to dark imaginings. Bachelard suggested that the correct relationship was in the form of a house as a 'vertical being', with the world of everyday activities placed at ground level to create a tripartite division of both space and phenomenological content.

Small houses that lack vertical organization still sometimes achieve this cave/pavilion polarity by the placement of a solid-walled service core within a framed structure, as in Frank Lloyd Wright's Usonion Houses – Wright was vehemently opposed to both cellars and attics. The little house near Talca in Chile designed by Smiljan Radic has neither, but within its 22 square metres (240 square feet) it manages to evoke the dual aspect of cave and pavilion by being at once both dug into and raised above the ground. The single-roomed structure is set into the side of a steep slope; it has a rectangular plan in which two walls are solid grey-and-green local granite. The entrance façade is part masonry with opening clerestory windows and a fully glazed door, while the fourth elevation looking down the hill comprises floor-to-ceiling glazed units set within a yellow-painted steel frame.

This page
The house is dug
into a steep slope
on the side of a
wooded valley.

Right
The main façade
is fully glazed and
supported by a
steel frame.

Above left
The solid end wall
is constructed of
unworked stone.

Above
The entrance door with
high-level ventilation
panels overhead.

Left
The house is both a
'cave' and a 'pavilion'.

The proportions of the space follow strict geometric principles, acknowledged to be based on Le Corbusier's modular method of dimensioning, but actually founded on a far older system of proportioning – that of the golden mean. At 3.66 x 5.92 metres (10½ x 19½ feet) the ratio of the length to the width of the house is 1.6176, the ratio used since before the classical Greek period to define the composition of all sacred buildings. In this house the golden mean also applies to the width-to-height ratio. The glazed panels are arranged as a series of squares, the generative shape of the golden mean itself.

Services are confined to each end of the space. By the entrance door is a small kitchen with a free-standing wood-fired oven and a timber worktop with a sink. The stove provides hot water through a heat-exchanging coil. The storage tank and pipework form a sculptural element that offsets the orthogonal geometry of the rest of the room. At the other end of the space, against the other stone wall, is an open shower and a wicker-lined timber cubicle containing a lavatory. The floor and ceiling are made of rough-sawn local timber throughout.

The roof – an extension of the natural terrace that runs along the hill – is a timber observation deck. Apart from stunning views of the ravine below and the distant mountains, the deck provides some of the necessities for outdoor living: an outside shower, a table and a brick barbecue.

Right
The roof acts
as a sundeck.

Far right
The landscape is
conceived as
being an extension
of the house.

Below left
The stone retaining wall
adjacent to the kitchen.

Below right
Facilities are basic
with heating and
cooking provided by
a wood burning oven.

Opposite page
Not immediately evident,
the proportioning of the
house is based on the
golden mean.

Above left
The virtually blank
entrance façade.

Above
A glazed strip
runs the entire
length of the ridge.

Left
Louvre panel in
open position.

Right
Solid interior
partitions act as
heat capacitors
utilizing solar gain.

Above
Views of the living
space — Sky House
is essentially all roof.

Right
Looking down from the
viewing gallery.

The very simple plan form has two bedrooms and a bathroom to the north side of the house, separated from the living space by a mass concrete wall 180 millimetres (7 inches) thick that acts as a heat sink in the otherwise timber structure. The wall gains heat from the sun during the day and radiates it back into the rooms at night. The external walls are clad in black-painted plywood, and the internal walls are lined in untreated shuttering ply, with 200 millimetres (8 inches) of mineral-wool insulation in the void. The east and west façades are fully glazed, with full-height louvre panels to control the amount of solar gain (Denmark has low sun angles for much of the year).

In the very centre of the house, accessible by an open stair, is a small first-floor deck that acts as an observation balcony – a feature that also figured strongly in the central glazed space of Villa Vision.

The original concept drawings of this house make it clear that Skude was influenced by the forms of structures from cultures that do not recognize the distinction between buildings and architecture. But Sky House speaks of the future and new forms of sustainable living rather than the past. The primary influence on its design seems to have been the work of Skude's fellow countryman Jørn Utzon, whose own houses on Majorca draw heavily on North

African and South American examples, in which walls are monolithic and rarely penetrated by windows. Skude's little house has the presence of an Aztec temple and the geometrical purity of an ancient ziggurat. It dispenses with the problem of how to articulate walls by presenting itself entirely as roof - and, in doing so, it can be seen as being either as temporary as a tent or as permanent as a rocky outcrop.

Early twentieth-century Modernists took a narrow view of the concept of function – in many cases, it was reduced to a materialistic perception of human needs, in which only the crudest interpretations of cooking, eating and sleeping informed architecture. In what became known as functionalism, architecture's ancient role to make consciously symbolic representations was forgotten or ignored. In his book *Places of the Soul,* Christopher Day describes this role as providing aesthetic nourishment, and he quotes the view of the Austrian philosopher Rudolf Steiner (1861–1925) that there is 'as much lying and crime in the world as there is lack of art'.

Steiner's complaint implies that there is a direct link between the artistic content of our environment and our individual sense of social responsibility and moral judgment. Making architecture a positive force for social change, in which artistic and purely practical values reinforce each other, is an approach that Day has referred to as 'spiritual functionalism'. The methodology for spiritual functionalism was inspired primarily by the scientific work of Johann Wolfgang von Goethe, particularly his researches into the metamorphosis of form in the natural world. For Goethe, what we see in plant formation, for example, is nothing other than an infinite number of variations on what he called the archetypal plant, or Ur-

Right
The tiny house evolved out of a former pigsty.

Far right
The curves of the outer walls are not just about aesthetics – they allow a tractor to turn into the field.

Right and below
Detailing is the result
of the act of making.

Right
Windows, kitchen
fittings and doors
are all hand-crafted.

organismus. This essentially holistic view relates directly to the creation of organic architectural forms, or Ur-forms – for, once discovered, these provide the basis not only of different forms for different functions in different environments but also for every detail within those forms. According to this philosophy, the building should literally grow out of the forces that form it, and the architect's role is that of an enabler with sufficient sensitivity to understand exactly what these forces are and how to give them positive expression.

Penllyn Fach had its origins both in a pigsty and in the ancient Celtic form of the roundhouse. Pen-y-Lyn, its larger neighbour, where Day still lives, takes the form of a traditional Welsh long house. In the 1980s the remaining walls of the original pigsty were extended and roofed to create a tractor shed. The gentle curve of the eastern wall reflects the turning circle of a tractor and trailer entering the field beyond. Then, in the mid-1990s, work was carried out to transform the space into a small house comprising a ground-floor living space and an attic bedroom accessible by ladder. The bathroom is in the main house, directly over the other side of the small entrance court to the south (until well into the twentieth century, most country cottages lacked internal lavatories).

Virtually all the materials used in the construction of Penllyn Fach are recycled or from the site. The stones, a form of Preseli granite, were carried there from nearby fields; the roof slates are second-hand; the timber was bought from reclamation yards; and the hardwood for the ladder was grown in the garden. The roof insulation is straw treated with borax – this, combined with the vermiculite and lime mix to the inner surface of the massive walls, means a very energy efficient space that can be heated by a single small wood-burning stove.

House in Hellschen

Germany 1996
Klaus Sill
110m² (1180 sq ft)

Right
In a flat landscape,
the form of the house
creates a protected
external space.

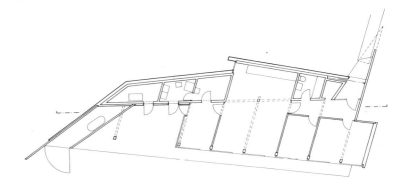

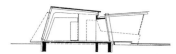

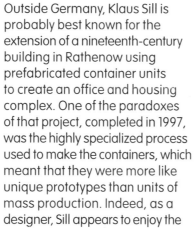

Outside Germany, Klaus Sill is probably best known for the extension of a nineteenth-century building in Rathenow using prefabricated container units to create an office and housing complex. One of the paradoxes of that project, completed in 1997, was the highly specialized process used to make the containers, which meant that they were more like unique prototypes than units of mass production. Indeed, as a designer, Sill appears to enjoy the possibilities inherent in prefabricated elements only in so far as they can be used as part of a rich and complex form language – in contrast with the normal tendency of industrial processes to reduce diversity and elaboration of form.

The French semiologist Roland Barthes argued in the 1960s that during the twentieth century human beings had moved from a world that was formed to a world that was assembled. To counter the deadening effects of industrialization, we must learn how to use its products to reinvest the built environment with complexity and difference, in a way that mirrors the natural world. This small house in the marshlands of Dithmarschen near the north coast of Germany illustrates how this aim might be achieved.

The landscape in this part of Germany is flat and exposed, dominated by the sky and the horizon. Even the trees remain

Above
Sequence of sections
at intervals along the
length of the house.

Top right
Plan.

Bottom right
The South façade
is fully glazed while
the north entrance
side is monolithic.

relatively small in the sandy soil – everything has a sense of the ephemeral, as if nothing, including the buildings, can take proper root. For an architect, the critical factor in such a case is how to provide protection from the elements and establish a sense of place. To meet the challenge, Sill has given the house in Hellschen two distinct sides and reinforced this conceptual device by the method of construction and the arrangement of rooms.

The exposed north side of the house is made of blockwork clad externally in aluminium panels; inside is a series of small service rooms and stores which act as a buffer between the main rooms and the outside environment. The façade is canted at 10 degrees from the vertical to give it the appearance of a medieval buttress. The service wall extends beyond the main rooms to provide external stores and tank rooms, and, more importantly, to protect a sun deck on the other side. The south-facing living room, bedrooms and workroom are contained within a timber frame, with laminated half-portals supporting a lightweight roof and fully glazed external wall.

Although the external form might suggest otherwise, the house is organized on a regular module defined by the grid of the timber portals, which allow removal or repositioning of partition walls between the main rooms. The house uses solar gain from the canted glazed façade to supplement heating, with external blinds to control the sunlight. The monolithic construction of the north side and the cast-concrete floor slab act as a heat sink to reduce energy consumption further.

Left
Standard components, like the windows, are used in non-repetitive ways to produce visual variety.

Top
The highly expressive entrance canopy viewed from the north and east.

Opposite page
The living room
looking towards the
terrace via the study.

Far left
Interior detailing
also utilizes catalogue
parts inventively.

Left
Solar façade – the floor
acts as a heat sink.

Bottom left
Kitchen with slot
window looking
towards the road.

Bottom right
View from the
entrance hall.

Above
The house replaces
an earlier cabin of the
same size.

Right
Sections. The roof
space contains the
sleeping platforms.

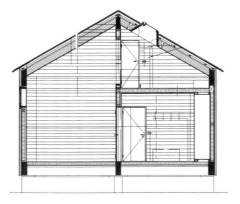 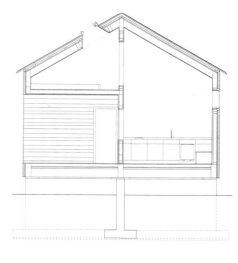

More than any other building type, the small house requires invention and skill to become building art and to contribute to architecture's continuing internal discourse. Ingenious solutions are often born of a combination of onerous restrictions such as a tight budget, a complex site and inflexible local planning regulations. Buildings that are ill conceived, weak in ideas and crudely developed have usually suffered from a lack of external pressures, resulting in a failure to tease out clear design principles.

The Summer Cabin was originally designed to replace another cabin on the same hillside site that had been destroyed by fire. The client wanted to enjoy the spectacular mountain panoramas, but the local planning authority insisted that the replacement should be the same size as the original, and that it should have the same ratio of wall to window openings – meaning, in practical terms, very few windows. The design solution was a square plan, notionally divided into quarters by cruciform foundations, in which one of the sub squares is an open south-facing deck that can be closed off externally by two sliding timber doors, thereby rendering the house virtually windowless.

Top
Cabin with sliding door closed.

Middle
With sliding door open revealing terrace.

Right
The landscape reflected in the picture window.

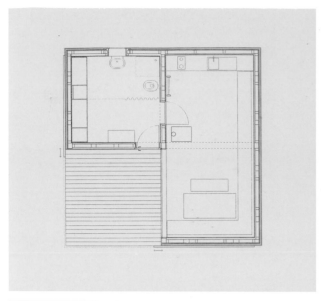

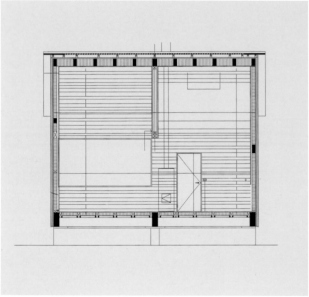

Above
Ground-floor plan
and long section
showing timber
frame construction.

Right top
Kitchen with the
access ladder to the
sleeping platforms.

Right middle and bottom
Views of the
sleeping platform.

The living space occupies half the ground floor, with a combined bathroom and entrance lobby taking up the third quarter. There are two sleeping spaces in the roof space over the sundeck and the bathroom, reached by a ladder from the kitchen. One is private and self-contained, while the other is an open gallery overlooking the kitchen. The roof comprises simply supported rafters between the central and the outer walls, allowing the living space to rise to double height. The four-part division of the plan is strictly adhered to, and reappears in the high-level partition that separates the kitchen from the living room.

There is no free-standing furniture in the cabin apart from the dining table; a built-in bench, a stainless-steel kitchen and a storage unit in the bathroom are the only elements seen to be indispensable. The house is heated by a wood-burning stove, centrally positioned to serve as both a functional and a symbolic focus.

Valentin Bearth worked for Peter Zumthor in Chur before setting up practice with Andrea Deplazes; their common emphasis on making particular buildings seemingly out of a single material is apparent in the cabin. When closed, the cabin appears to be made entirely of timber. Zumthor's Gugalin House (1994), an extension to an eighteenth-century 'Strickbauten', or 'knitted building', also exemplifies this approach. By virtue of their butt-jointed details and precise ordering, both buildings appear to have been carved out of a solid material rather than assembled from individual components.

Left
The living space
comprises a
dining table with
fixed seating.

Ithaca House
New York State, USA, 2000
Simon Ungers
90m² (970 sq ft)

Writing in the introduction to his book The Shingle Style Today (1974), Vincent Scully describes Le Corbusier's Villa Savoye in the following way: 'It is a closed system, complete. Inside, it is the hermetic labyrinth of the mind, the special world of Cubism, of man-made forms pursuing the circuitous paths of intellectual quest, infinitely overlapping. And that internal universe, that volume encased as in one of Leonardo's skulls by its thin external shell, is set in its exact opposite: in the Impressionist landscape, the world of nature loved for itself in the light that reveals it, Monet's world of empirical external reality.' The North American shingle style could be viewed as that continent's version of National Romanticism, and Scully, in this piece of writing, is trying to reconcile this architectural style with the move in the 1980s towards more geometric and pure forms. What Scully refers to as a 'classicizing' of design has its origins in the earlier history of the settlement of North America. Lacking a cultural context (the indigenous one of the North American Indians was effectively annihilated), architects turned to Europe and Classical Greece as the model for the buildings and layouts of planned cities like Washington, as if in an unconscious attempt to authenticate the values of a people who as yet had no history. This level of abstraction found added force in a view that set nature up in opposition to human progress and described all interactions with it in terms of combat – nature had to be conquered, subdued, overcome, and ultimately made to deliver on terms set by people, not the environment.

Above
The house has abstract formal qualities that place it in opposition to the landscape.

Above
The monolithic appearance is achieved through careful proportioning and choice of materials.

Left
Ground- and first-floor plans. The external stair leads to a roof terrace.

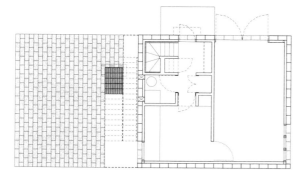

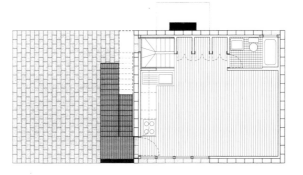

Above
First-floor living space.

Cologne-based architect Simon Ungers clearly enjoys the abstract qualities inherent in overtly geometric forms placed in a natural landscape. Although small, particularly by American standards, the Ithaca House has presence by virtue of its rectilinear form and visual density of its closely laid concrete blockwork walls. The apparently random arrangement of external openings for windows and doors amplifies its monolithic characteristics and gives it gravitas in spite of its diminutive size.

There are just two internal levels of accommodation – on the ground floor a studio and garage, and above that a single-roomed apartment. The roof is a terrace that is accessible by an external stair connecting the upper levels to the ground. The deceptively simple detailing is designed to produce visually minimalist surfaces. The hollow block external walls, 200 millimetres (8 inches) thick, have thin 9 millimetres (½ inch) raked mortar joists and are lined with a softwood

frame 100 millimetres (4 inches) deep filled with rigid insulation to give better than average thermal performance. Oak skirtings and architraves are set flush with the plasterboard lining.

The house is conceived as being the first phase of a larger project which compounds the paradoxes surrounding its design: an object building that is incomplete; formal yet with randomly composed openings; stripped of all

unnecessary features but somehow aesthetically generous. The house exists on the knife-edge duality of freedom and fundamentalism, in a perfect mirror of the ambiguities of its cultural context – the USA.

Above
The detailing allows
each surface to exist
as a pure plane.

Villa Eila
Guinea, West Africa 1995
Mikko Heikkinen
and Markku Komonen
75m² (810 sq ft)

Below
Plan with
landscape
features.

Right
The house sits
on a terrace on
a gentle slope.

The Finnish architects Mikko Heikkinen and Markku Komonen have worked on several other buildings apart from the Villa Eila in or near the small town of Mali, including a clinic (1994), a village school (1997) and a poultry farm (1998). All these buildings were initiated by Eila Kivekås, the founder of the Indigo Association, whose primary aim is to promote women's vocational training in the area. The name Indigo comes from the local method of dyeing fabric – a task that remains the responsibility of women master dyers, who use traditional techniques to produce a unique deep indigo colour.

Although Villa Eila is a private house, it is also used by Finnish workers involved in the Indigo Association's programmes. The ethos of the association is very much reflected in these buildings – it seeks not to impose the values of post-industrial northern Europe but to work with existing resources to empower the local people in ways that preserve their culture and customs. Historically, foreign interventions in Central Africa have had a generally destructive influence. In building, the widespread use of concrete and profiled metal have made traditional, ecologically sound construction techniques all but redundant. But projects such as Villa Eila and work

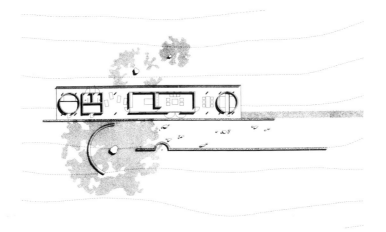

by such groups as Intermediate Technology show a new sensitivity towards the issue of aid, education and health in some of the poorest countries in the world (adult life expectancy in Guinea is about forty years).

In northern Guinea, firing bricks is prohibited by law to protect the endangered forests, but stopping it is difficult, and in the uplands many buildings are constructed with fired bricks. Villa Eila is made of unburned bricks of stabilized earth. This involved careful selection of local soils mixed with about 5 per cent cement at a precise moisture content; the mixture was then formed into individual bricks in a manual press, one brick at a time. The roof tiles were also made locally by a similar technique but with slightly more cement and sisal-fibre reinforcement to strengthen the thin profiled sections. A clay-tile floor and bamboo screens meant that all the basic components of the house were not only made from local materials using local labour but dispensed with the need for on-site electricity for power tools and machinery.

The house stands on one side of a valley, with its monopitch roof matching that of the slope. Under the continuous form of the roof are a series of self-contained rooms, each of which can be seen as a tiny separate house in its own right. Between these formally composed rooms – they are squares, circles or rectangles – are closed verandas protected from the sun by bamboo screens. Below the house is a stone terrace with a semicircular bench built facing a large tree, in recognition of the unique features of the place.

Left
Floor tiles and
unburnt bricks
were made on site.

Right
The house is a series
of rooms connected by
roofed but open spaces.

Far right
Detailing is a
combination of the
raw and the cooked.

Right middle
The west elevation with
typical cross-section
shown beside.

Far right middle
Bamboo screens protect
the rooms from the sun.

Bottom
The construction
incorporated
traditional crafts.

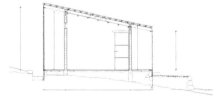

Small House

Tokyo, Japan 2000
Kazuyo Sejima
76m² (820 sq ft)

Right
The form is a particular
response to the site.

The world's most densely populated cities are Hong Kong, Moscow and Tokyo, parts of which have more than 1000 people per hectare (400 people per acre). These figures are approaching the highest density ever recorded, in Lower East Side Manhattan at the end of the nineteenth century in the so-called Dumb-bell tenements, which contained a staggering 1350 people per hectare (540 people per acre).

Kazuyo Sejima has had plenty of experience of designing compact houses for extremely restricted sites. One of her most inventive solutions was S-House in Okayama prefecture, completed in 1996, which is contained within an outer envelope of polycarbonate sheeting that filters the immediate external environment. As a designer, she is unsentimental about the role of architecture, preferring to see it as reflecting current cultural values rather than presenting competing visions of what ought to be. Maintaining this position requires a fine balance between cynicism and romanticism.

The Small House is a miniature tower embodying many of the ideas that makes Sejima's position so pertinent today. First, the infill site of 60 square metres (650 square feet) at the end of a cul-de-sac had an allowable building footprint of only 36 square metres (390 square feet) and required an inventive and radical solution to the brief of providing permanent accommodation for a couple and their young daughter. Second, the house reflects the persistent interest in stacking – as seen in the Kitagata public housing in Gifu prefecture, completed in 1994, but here allied to a spatial dynamic that allows each floor a degree of autonomy. Third, the relationship between public and private space within the context of the individual dwelling was of prime importance.

The accommodation is organized on four levels. A semi-basement provides a sleeping place, with daylight coming from a narrow courtyard against the adjacent property. The upper ground floor

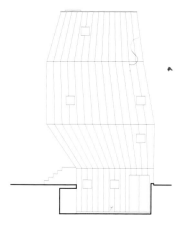

Above
Offsets in section are made possible by a steel frame.

Right
Cladding is galvanized steel or glazed panels.

Far right
Each floor is relatively autonomous.

combines an entrance hall with a space reserved for guests, and above this is the equivalent of a 'piano nobile' for living, cooking and dining. The top floor is occupied by an open-plan bathroom and an enclosed roof terrace that has views to the west across a vacant building site. [Within this apparently precise division of functions, the position of the child is ambiguous – having no designated space of her own but being seen rather as a nomad within the entire house].

The compact upper ground floor has room for car parking, while the living space above is significantly larger and has a proportionately higher ceiling. The tapered top floor minimizes the restriction of daylight to surrounding buildings and visually terminates the composition.

An open steel shaft containing the spiral stair supports the concrete floor plates. At the perimeter the floors are supported on slender steel columns that follow the building profile. The envelope is approximately 50 per cent glazed, primarily to the west, and 50 per cent covered in galvanized-steel panels with articulated standing seams. As with other Sejima projects, the envelope is seen as a stretched skin, barely concealing the activities of the inhabitants from public gaze.

Top
Top floor with open-plan bathroom.

Above
Main living floor with high ceiling.

Above
Floors are propped off
the central spiral stair.

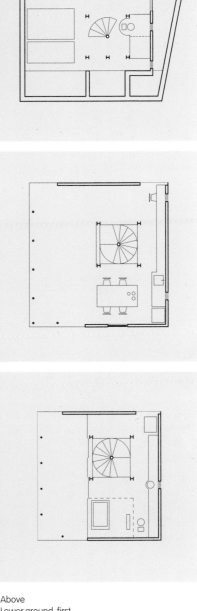

Above
Lower ground, first
and second floors.

Louis Kahn (1901–74) kept a book of European castle plans close to his desk. In his later projects, in particular, there is a fascination with the possibilities of the thick wall, hollowed out to accommodate a series of small cells, surrounding a large internal space. The parliamentary buildings in Dhaka, dating from the last decade of Kahn's life, have this medieval quality of solidity and mass. Over successive eras, architecture has been about the reduction of material substance. Look at the ground plan of an Egyptian temple – it is more than 50 per cent matter, reflecting a view of space as full, and of enclosure as something created by the removal or hollowing out of stone. We have now arrived at the opposite pole: space is considered to be empty, and architecture is formed by placing thin planes in the emptiness to produce envelopes often no thicker than sheets of glass. It is difficult to reproduce the sensation of density – particularly in domestic architecture, where the scale of the architectural elements is reduced.

Jun Tamaki has recently designed two houses that capture a sense of density: House Hakama and Villa Tofu, both in Kyoto. Outwardly their appearance is similarly monolithic, but House Hakama is for a family and has two levels of accommodation, while Villa Tofu is for an elderly couple and is organized on one level only. Villa Tofu occupies a restricted site, with a small park in a square at the front. Within a rectangular plan form, a zone of service rooms is wrapped around three sides of the building; these contain the entrance hall, kitchen, store room, bathroom and utility room. In addition, deep window reveals have been cut through this wall of rooms, creating alcoves. All the main functions – dining, living, sleeping – take place in the central linear space that has a ceiling height of 3.6 metres (12 feet) and which is subdivisible by sliding screens. At the front end of this temple-like volume is a deep bay window with splayed reveals that gives a view of the park. From outside, this aperture is the only

Right
Plan. The house is conceived as one central space surrounded by a thick wall of ancillary rooms.

Far right
View of the entrance from the square.

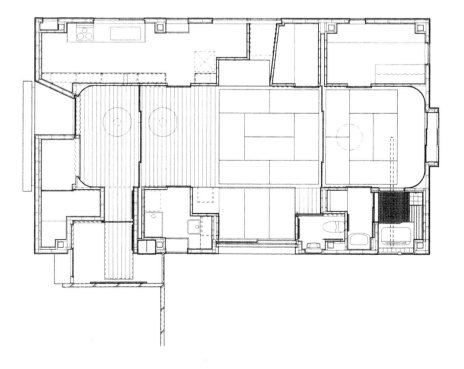

articulation of the front façade; it is carefully detailed so that the supporting steel frame to the sliding sash is invisible from the street, thereby maintaining a continuity of surface from outside to inside. The theme of continuity persists inside, where all the doors are sliding doors hung to resemble monochrome paintings on the otherwise completely white walls, which have the same texture and finish as the external ones.

The main core space has virtually no free-standing furniture, and two thirds of the floor is covered in tatami mats. The large dividing screens, set at both low and high levels, slide back into deep slots in the perimeter walls. Also within these walls, like sedilias in a church, are small recesses for displaying treasured objects, including a vertical slot for a fifty-year-old book on Henri Matisse, the only book in the house.

The thick perimeter walls – made from rendered lath fixed onto a supporting steel frame – are in fact hollow. The steel becomes apparent only at roof level, where the gutter and deep eaves soffit are in exposed metal.

Above
The occupants' only book has a specially designed slot to house it.

Above
The ancillary rooms comprise the kitchen, bathroom and storage.

Above
View of the alcove
with garden beyond.

Top
Deep windows cut
through the perimeter
wall and allow light into
the living space.

Above
Looking from the main
space towards the front
of the house.

Right
The house is cut into a
bank that once was the
site of two garages.

The term 'brownfield site' is used to designate a previously developed piece of land that has become redundant in terms of its former function. Planning legislation in Europe over the past ten years has favoured brownfield sites over greenfield sites for new-build projects. But the enactment of this policy, particularly in the UK, has been hindered by the conservatism of local planning authorities. In England, gaining consent to redevelop such sites often entails overcoming a series of seemingly intractable obstacles and persuading a string of interested parties.

Studio House occupies part of a conservation area in the cathedral town of Winchester. The wide but shallow site had previously contained two prefabricated lock-up garages. Richard Rose-Casemore and his partner bought it speculatively, then set about trying to satisfy the authorities. Convincing conservation officers that contemporary designs are contextual can be extremely difficult, particularly in a country where pseudo-vernacular alternatives are still seen as preferable. In this part of Winchester the nearby terraces are early Edwardian – modestly elegant and with a strong visual language of red brickwork, bay windows and steep gables.

The proposal for a small house that would cut into the existing bank, with a screen wall to the lower level shielding it from the street and a fully glazed southeast-facing street façade, did not meet with the planning authorities' approval and attracted numerous letters of objection from local residents. However, the scheme was allowed to go forward for consideration by the planning committee, which – very unusually in such circumstances – voted to approve the project. The time between land purchase and occupation of Studio House was approximately three years; the process was not helped when the contractor went into liquidation halfway through construction.

Left
Diagrammatic
isometric of the main
constructional elements.

Below
The screenwall
conceals a small
courtyard garden.

Below
View via the courtyard
gate off the street.

Right
Entrance to main living
floor is via the bank.

Above
Because of the context,
the house had difficulty
gaining a permission
to build.

Above
The second lower-
level courtyard.

Above
The upper-level
living space.

The organization of the house is a response to the constraints of the site. The lower level, containing the bedroom, service rooms and a workroom, is dug into the bank and protected by a concrete and blockwork retaining wall. The rooms open out on one side only to a walled courtyard adjacent to the pavement. Entry to the house is at the upper level, a one-volume mezzanine from which a steel stair leads down to the lower level. The shallow monopitch roof has high-level glazing over the rear wall, but otherwise the living room looks exclusively southeast over the surrounding mature gardens and distant views of the city. A steel frame means that there are no load-bearing internal walls.

Although the house looks like an individually designed, high-budget project, the building costs were about average for a conventional small house. This was achieved by using a number of standard industrial components such as the roof lights and curtain walling, and selected recycled items such as a stainless-steel worktop.

Top
The stair well effectively makes the upper level a mezzanine.

Above
Detailing utilizes many standard components.

Above
Lower-level study.

House in a
Suitcase
Barcelona, Spain 2001
Eva Prats and Ricardo Flores
27m² (290 sq ft)

Right
The single volume top
lit space measures
just 3m x 3m x 9m
(10 x 10 x 30 ft).

Below
Plan with sections.
The apartment sits
on the roof of an
existing block of flats.

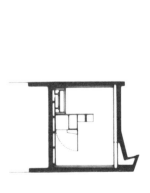

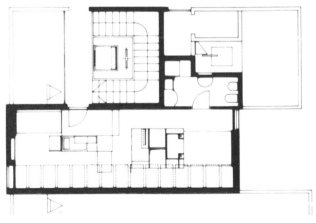

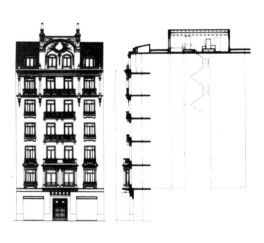

Modernism engendered a certain kind of obsession with putting things away. In an age increasingly dominated by the photographic image, the term 'messy' came to be used to describe what had previously been the necessary result of everyday activity. Progressive dependence on technology supported this aesthetic, as houses became sites of consumption rather than production. Western materialistic thinking demands clear categories, but clutter, in that it defies categorization of objects, threatens this narrow view of order. However, Gaston Bachelard looked at the latent possibilities of drawers, chests and wardrobes in his book The Poetics of Space (1958) and found that they are 'veritable organs of the secret psychological life'. According to this phenomenological reading, the idea of hiding things nourishes our daydreams. In her book A Hut of One's Own (1997), Ann Cline examines the history of cabinets, which were originally for an eclectic range of items, both natural and man-made. Only in the eighteenth century did rationalists begin to insist on cataloguing the contents of such pieces of furniture.

Two seminal twentieth-century artists who subverted the role of the container were Marcel Duchamp and Joseph Beuys. After completing The Large Glass, Duchamp spent much of the late 1930s making a piece called The Box in a Valise, in which all his work was reproduced in miniature, as in a travelling art gallery. Beuys produced many works in which the relationship between the contained and the container was ambiguous – for example, I know no weekend (1972) is a readymade object in which a black briefcase contains a carefully mounted bottle of sauce and a copy of Immanuel Kant's Critique of Pure Reason. Architecture lacks the potential to be ironic, succeeding normally in offering new readings of reality only by default.

Flores's and Prats's design for a temporary home on the roof of a Barcelona apartment block, executed without irony, takes the idea of ordering possessions to its logical conclusion. The single-roomed space measures 3 x 3 x 9 metres (10 x 10 x 30 feet), plus a small shower room to one side. The primary source of daylight is a linear roof light that runs the entire length of one side of the room – indicating that the experience of occupying the room is intended to be internalized. Two purpose-designed timber trunks contain all the facilities deemed necessary for the room's periodic use. Although fairly crudely detailed in laminated ply, each trunk has a complex series of folding and sliding elements that enables it to be transformed for different uses. When the room is unoccupied, they act as protective packing cases for a limited range of belongings.

The bedroom 'trunk' has a pull-out double bed, clothes-hanging space, bedside tables, mirror and linen cupboard, plus compartments for more precious objects. The kitchen 'trunk' is backed up against a slightly raised entrance level; as well as a stainless-steel mini-kitchen, it contains a fold-out table and hinged shelf that close the unit when it is not in use. A spare bed pulls out from under the void of the raised floor by the front door. The iconography is that of the display unit, suggesting that, within this particular vision, living and shopping are virtually synonymous.

Top left and right
Room with the
'suitcases' both
closed and open.

Above left and right
A place for anything
and everything in
its place.

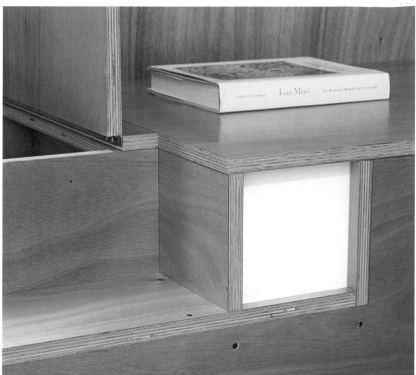

Top left and right
The wardrobe screens
the sleeping area.

Above left and right
The bed slides away
when not required.

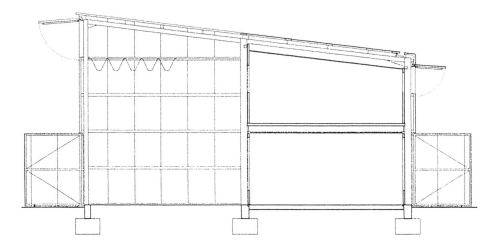

Above right
Typical section.

Many architects and designers are ill-equipped to work within small budgets, since they have been trained in a discipline driven by bourgeois expectations and aspirations that has historically put aesthetics before money. Attempts to create a designed vernacular – a contradiction in terms – often end up either as pieces of unthinking sentimentality or as over-intellectualized icons that destroy the integrity of their source material. The essential difference between the vernacular tradition and consciously designed work is that the vernacular lacks abstraction; its ideas are about action rather than commentary.

Lacaton's and Vassal's work is important because it deals with this difficult area unambiguously. Their small domestic projects of the past decade have generally been executed on tight budgets for clients who would not normally employ architects. The methodology for conceiving and making these buildings is consistent – the use of standard, readily available components in inventive ways. The aesthetic is derived from the vernacular agricultural buildings of Europe, whose function is to offer maximum volume for minimum cost.

Designed for a couple with two children, Maison Latapie is in an inner suburb of Bordeaux, an area of ordinary one- and two-storey houses lining quiet side streets. The basic structural system is a steel frame, as in a prefabricated warehouse or barn, clad in profiled fibre cement panels fixed to horizontal purlins. On the street side, this cladding comprises both fixed and hinged elements; when all these movable panels are closed, the façade becomes a wall of uninterrupted sheeting with no apparent glazing or means of access.

On the east side, facing the garden, is a lightweight steel-framed polycarbonate-clad conservatory that has a volume greater than the house itself. Plywood doors and windows open up the main rooms to this space, so that, although it offers the minimum of environmental control, it is an integral part of the otherwise small house and usable for most of the year. Without fixed edges, the accommodation offers a constantly changing backdrop to the domestic routine, sometimes intimate and protective, sometimes expansive and exposed.

The plan organization on two floors reflects this philosophy. There are no rooms as such; the spaces are defined by the position of the service core containing the kitchen, bathroom and stair. Internally, the finishes make maximum use of sheet timber, which avoids wet trades and reduces construction time. This insulated timber box, with its external doors and shutters, is inserted into the steel frame and forms the innermost part of the layered envelope of what is a deceptively simple house.

Below
Sequence showing
the opening up of
the street façade.

Bottom
View of the
polycarbonate
conservatory from
the garden.

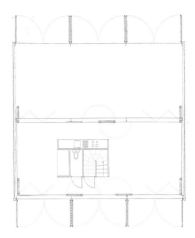

Above
Ground-floor and
first-floor plan.

Above
The conservatory is
larger than the house.

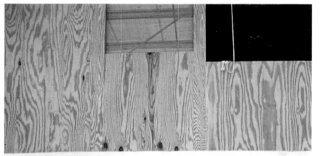

Above
The living space is
connected to the
conservatory via
simply constructed
sliding doors.

Top
The house imposes
no particular lifestyle
on the inhabitants.

Above
The interior lining
is shuttering ply.
Materials are common-
place and inexpensive.

Kern House

Lochau, Austria 1997
Carlo Baumschlager
and Dietmar Eberle
First-floor apartment:
90m² (300 sq ft)

Sensational sites gifted by generous parents have been the basis of a number of iconic twentieth-century houses – for example, the Tugendhat House in Brno, Czech Republic, designed by Mies van der Rohe, and the Maison de Verre in Paris designed by Pierre Chareau, both of 1933. The Kern House was designed for the daughter and granddaughter of the owners of a large site – a gently sloping hill of open grassland dotted with trees – overlooking Lake Constance on the borders of Germany, Switzerland and Austria. Baumschlager and Eberle located the building near other residences to allow an open aspect to the south and west and to avoid blocking existing views down the hill.

The house is organized on two floors, with the ground floor given over to a garage, a guest room and space for coats and boots. All the main living accommodation is on the first floor, which is arranged as one large open-plan space with two small bedrooms at one end. Kitchen and bathroom are cantilevered boxes attached to the north side of the house, lit only by roof lights.

The envelope is designed both to exploit the possibilities of the views and to maintain privacy. The house has two skins. An inner membrane is supported by a pinewood frame infilled with sheathed and insulated panels, mainly timber, on the north and east sides, and glass on the south and west. The outer skin comprises a gridded timber frame on which are set horizontal slats of larchwood, arranged in sections to render the skin progressively more transparent the higher up the building it goes. Sliding glazed units set at regular intervals in the inner skin act as floor-to-ceiling windows, with their corresponding slats forming top-hung shutters in the outer surface. At the west end of the main living space is an internal terrace, partially screened by the slats and shutters, giving it the quality of an outside room with a carefully controlled view of the lake.

The outer skin acts as a constant reference matrix for the landscape as seen from the house, fragmenting it into a series of horizontal and vertical slices. This is a very contemporary view of landscape – painterly in the Renaissance tradition of the framed view but with the stratification of the pixilated image. The double skin also reintroduces to domestic architecture the possibilities inherent in the thick wall – in this example, approximately 600 millimetres (25 inches) thick.

The origins of the open horizontal-slat façade lie in the timber-drying sheds of Europe and the 'brise-soleil' of Mediterranean and Middle Eastern vernacular buildings. Used in conjunction with an inner, more substantial weather envelope, it achieves one of the fantasies of the Modern movement – a house made, apparently, of only one material that seamlessly covers the entire composition.

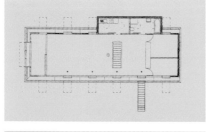

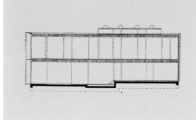

Above left
First-floor plan
and long section.

Above
Garden façade
with shutters open.

Above
At night the
transparency of the
house is more apparent.

Opposite page
Larch slats are
progressively open
towards the top of
the building giving
a combination of
privacy and views out.

Above
The access stair
to the apartment.

Top
The landscape is seen
against the matrix of
the outer skin.

Above
The void between the
inner and outer skins.

House on Twin Peaks

San Francisco, USA 1997
Ace Architects
150m² (1610 sq ft)

Below
Site plan with upper-ground-floor plan of the house.

Below right
Axonometric view with garage to the right.

Far right
House seen from the entrance side.

Robert Venturi's influential polemic *Complexity and Contradiction in Architecture* (1966) made a clear case for questioning the established tenets of 'the puritanically moral language of orthodox Modern architecture'. Venturi made an eloquent case for the hybrid rather than the pure, for the distorted rather than the straightforward, for the ambiguous rather than the articulated, the inconsistent and equivocal rather than the direct and clear. In short, he proclaimed himself to be 'for messy vitality over obvious unity'. Although American architects such as Charles Moore and Robert Sterne made successful careers from largely domestic projects that reflected Venturi's beliefs, large sections of the profession refused to accept the validity of an approach that they saw as populist and vulgar.

Likewise, the work of Ace Architects reflects broad references that sit outside the normal remit of architecture. Abstraction is avoided, and there is an obvious delight in representing a building's underlying influences, including the client's own likes and dislikes, very directly. In the House on Twin Peaks, the site, its history and the client's biography and interests have all been used to guide the building's form and detail.

On a wooded hillside overlooking downtown San Francisco, the large site already had various buildings on it, including a redwood cabin that the client's parents had built in the 1940s. Over time, a small cottage and a dairy barn, salvaged from an adjacent farm, had been added. The initial plan was to renovate and convert the barn to provide another self-contained and compact residence, but this idea was dropped

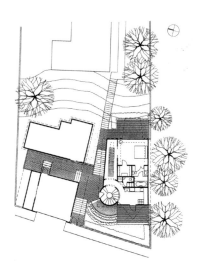

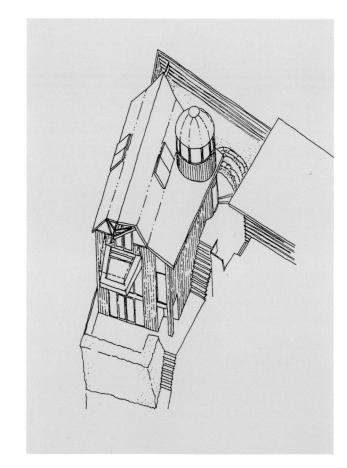

in favour of a new building that retained echoes of the original form. Immediately obvious visual references to the original are the gambrel roof and the circular stair tower modelled on a grain silo. A new flight of access steps leading down to the main house from the street links the buildings together and allows dramatic vistas through the cypress trees of the city and the bay below.

The house is on three levels, with the entrance on the middle floor. The attic, under the exposed timber framing of the roof, is a single living space terminated by a cantilevered balcony. Below is the main bedroom, bathroom and kitchen linked by a tapering gallery that breaks the orthogonal geometry of the underlying barnlike structure. This top-lit gallery has echoes of the tricks of perspective used by Sir John Soane in his own house in Lincoln's Inn Fields in London, begun in 1813. The ground floor contains a guest bedroom and study.

The vertical cedar boarding on the outside of the house contrasts with the horizontal boarding with pronounced cover battens used for the new garage and the fencing. Internally, the most spatially dynamic element is the spiral stair, finished in gold leaf and top-lit by means of extensive high-level glazing. Cutouts in its encompassing walls allow natural light into the deepest parts of the plan, reinforcing the impression that the house, small by North American standards, is projecting itself as a city in miniature, with cultural references from places as far apart as Mexico, Italy and Japan.

Top left
The stair tower.

Top right
View of the main bathroom from the bedroom.

Above
Dramatic cantilevered balcony with its views of the city below.

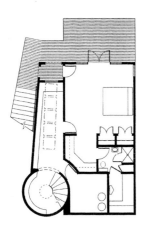

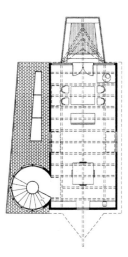

Top left
Lower ground
and attic plans.

Top and above
Views of the staircase.

Top and above
Views of the attic
living room.

Mews House
London, England 1997
Seth Stein
80m² (860 sq ft)

Right
From the mews
the house appears
almost conventional.

The inspiration for this small mews house in the Knightsbridge area of London was an episode of the TV series The Avengers called 'The House that Jack Built', in which the heroine Emma Peel is temporarily imprisoned in a country house, unable to find her way out of a particular pair of rooms no matter how many doors she opens. The secret Emma discovers is that the rooms move around one another mechanically while she is in them.

The impact of this scene depends on the fact that the technology – while making possible a seemingly impossible experience – remains an enabler rather than becoming the focus of attention. The architect Seth Stein likewise treats technology not as the generator of an aesthetic but rather as an invisible support to a highly complex series of spatial games. Although Stein has worked for both Richard Rogers and Norman Foster, his relationship to technology is in this sense more sophisticated than theirs.

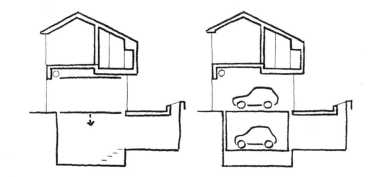

Above
Diagrammatic sections showing the operation of the car lift.

Below
Glass-bottomed car lift seen parked on the ground floor.

Below
The courtyard garden has roof lights that illuminate the dining room below.

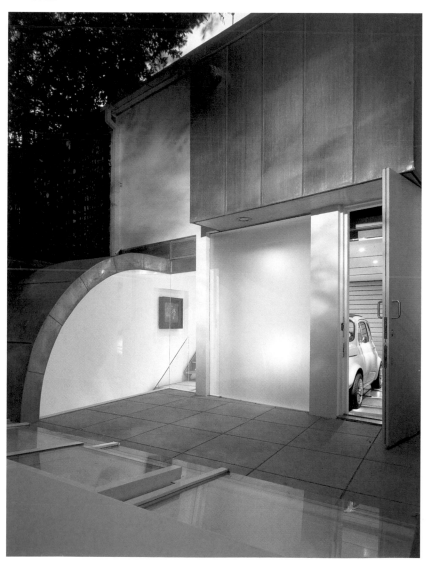

As with all really radical design solutions, this one had its roots in tight external restraints. The previously vacant site had an overall footprint of only 4.5 x 8.5 metres (15 x 28 feet), but the local planning regulations required that off-street parking be maintained and that the building rise no more than two floors above ground level. In addition, the frontage had to adhere to England's inflexible conservation regulations, which can effectively force a historical pastiche onto street façades in sensitive sites.

Stein's solution was to seize virtue from necessity by making the cars and their parking arrangements the central motif of the house – the design is for a double garage that has the facility to provide highly serviced living accommodation. The curve of the glass entrance door allows the cars to turn off the narrow mews and enter a double-decker car lift through a roller-shutter door. A new basement was excavated over the entire site to allow the lower car deck to descend below ground and the upper car deck to be stationed at street level. This seemingly simple concept is the mechanism that led to the creation of a dynamic series of spaces which not only expand the confines of the tiny site but allow most of the internal spaces to be transformed at the flick of a switch. When one or both cars are in place, they act as sculptural backdrops to everyday life (the client has a particular love of classic small Italian cars – specifically the Dante Giacosa-designed Fiat 500), but when the lift is empty its vacant decks become extensions of the living space. When the lift is lowered, the basement pit accommodates permanently placed furniture, but when the lift is raised this area is revealed as part of the kitchen and dining area. The bottom deck has acrylic panels set in a steel frame to give it transparency. A 'pocket' in the underside of the attic bedroom floor can also accommodate furniture on the top deck even when it is raised. Electrically controlled solid or glass partitions close off the lift whenever it is operated.

The three levels of the house are linked by a straight-flight glass stair that diffuses daylight from above and is aligned on a square window in the front façade to give a constant view of the sky. To the rear of the house, at ground level, is a small courtyard garden with a continuous roof light at low level along its rear flank wall, which washes the dining room beneath with natural light.

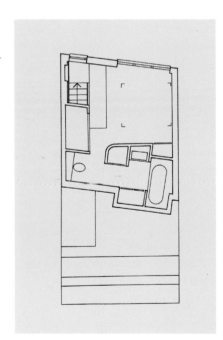
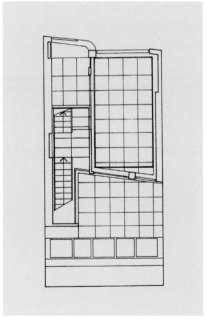
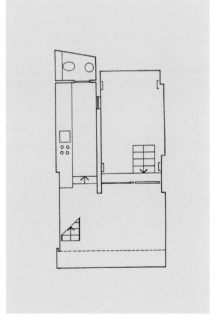

Above
Attic, ground and
basement level plans.

Right
In spite of its scale,
the house has great
visual depth.

Above
With the car lift raised,
the lower level of the
basement becomes
a living room.

Above
A straight-flight glass
stair creates a sense
of vertical expansion.

Above
View from the lift
pit towards the
dining room.

Above
Bespoke construction
extends to the
smallest of details.

Before embarking on the Morton Loft conversion, Ada Tolland and Giuseppe Lignano of LOT/EK Architects had already used the detritus of post-industrial society as a major element in the design of a small and radical living space. The basis for the Guzman Penthouse in New York was a redundant container truck placed on the roof of an eleven-storey residential block close to the Empire State Building. The modification and extension of the container, using steel as the main material, created a two-storey apartment of 110 square metres (1190 square feet) with its own garden on a tiny part of the largely uninhabited city roofscape. The design methodology consists in displacing, transforming and manipulating familiar objects in an attempt to create what the architects refer to as an 'artificial nature'.

An extreme example of this approach is found in a short story by J. G. Ballard, The Ultimate City, which describes the work of an architect called Buckmaster, an octogenarian visionary seemingly modelled on Buckminster Fuller: 'Rising from the centre of the square was the largest of the eccentric memorials to 20th century technology that Halloway had seen so far. At first glance it resembled a gothic cathedral, built entirely from rusting iron, glass and chromium. As they crossed the square, Halloway realised that this structure was built entirely of automobiles. Stacked one upon the other, they formed a palisade of towers that rose two hundred feet in the air.'

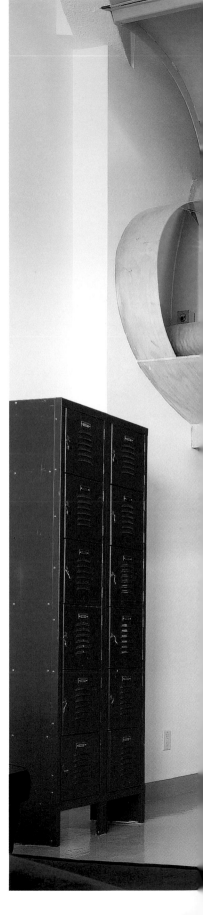

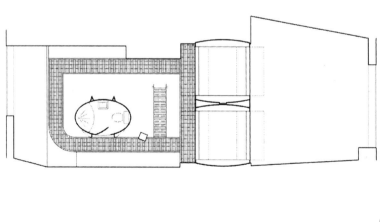

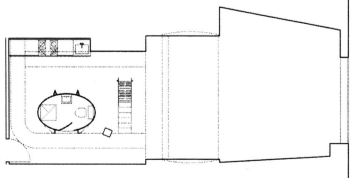

Left
Plans of the mezzanine (top) and main levels (bottom), showing the bathroom container on the left and the sleeping container on the right.

Right
A recycled petroleum trailer tank, cut into two pieces, forms the basis of the apartment organization. One tank houses sleeping compartments, the other the bathroom.

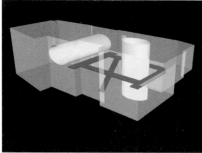

Top and right
Photographs showing the installation of the tanks in the fourth-floor apartment, itself created out of part of a former multi-storey parking garage.

Above
Axonometric illustration showing the placement of the tanks and gantries within the loft space.

Left and top
A bathroom within
the vertical tank –
the aesthetic is a
combination of the
refined and the crude.

Right
Access to the sleeping
compartments is
via resin-filled steel
metal mesh gantries.

Opposite page
Hydraulically assisted
hatches on the
bedroom tanks can
be opened for light
and air or closed
for privacy.

Automobiles figure heavily in the Morton Loft project. The building that houses this apartment on the fourth floor was originally a multi-storey car park. The double-height space has been converted using the trailer unit from a petroleum tanker, which was installed in two sections through the main window opening, using a mobile crane. One half of the bifurcated unit has been slung at high level across the middle of the apartment to provide two sleeping capsules. The other half has been placed vertically in the space and fitted with bathrooms on two levels. Its inherent strength means that the tank can clear-span the party walls without additional support. Although both sections have been heavily modified, it is obvious that the apartment is fashioned from materials that lie outside architecture's normal stock. The bed spaces have large, hydraulically operated, gull-wing doors cut into the tank for access, ventilation and daylight. Apart from their bright yellow paint finish, the bathrooms are deliberately designed to lack finesse – all the plumbing is face-fixed to the outsides of the tanks, and the larger piping has hose-clamp connections, as used in trucks and car-cooling systems.

Lightweight steel gantries, the type normally seen in factories, give access to the upper levels; the mesh in the floor plates is infilled with clear resin to give them a jewel-like semi-transparency when viewed from below and above. These elements and the stainless-steel kitchen unit contrast with the crude state of the building's original structure with its industrial-paint finish over the uneven concrete flooring of what was once the car-park deck.

Schretter Apartment
Vienna, Austria 1998
Eichinger, Oder, Knechtl
50m² (540 sq ft)

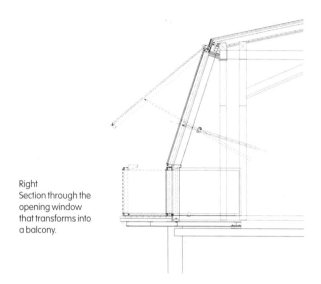

Right
Section through the
opening window
that transforms into
a balcony.

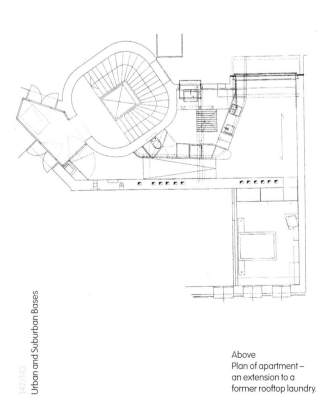

Urban and Suburban Bases

Above
Plan of apartment –
an extension to a
former rooftop laundry.

Gaston Bachelard, using a phenomenological reading and evoking literary references, argues that the cellar.is a place where the unconscious mind cannot be civilized whereas in the attic our fears can be quickly rationalized. The psychologist Carl Jung presents a similar picture when describing the design and construction of his own house at Bollingen by the Upper Lake of Zurich. Begun in 1922 but built in phases, the final part of the house was a small tower with a room at the top for what Jung called 'spiritual concentration'. Attics occupy a particular place in our collective imagination, as writers of children's stories know better than most. Peter Pan, the boy who could never grow old, lived a charmed life, often at rooftop level. Mary Poppins, who had many magical abilities, could fly and experience the city as if in a permanently floating attic removed from the material world.

The basis for the Schretter Apartment was an old rooftop laundry in a residential block. One conventional room at the same level was also available, and this has become the apartment's only bedroom. The roof of the laundry area was remodelled, and the timber trusses exposed internally. The one external wall, overlooking an inner courtyard, was removed and rebuilt with two large windows. The larger of these is a two-part unit: the top part hinges open to head height, while the bottom part slides forward to become a small balcony. Both units are electrically operated.

The potentially problematic L-shaped space was further restricted by the adjacent main stair, the line of chimney flues from the apartments below and the position of service drops. The architectural solution is ingenious. Apart from the given bedroom, there are no rooms as such; there is simply a single continuous space that can be configured in different ways through sliding and folding elements. Entry is through a large steel door that leads to a short passage flanked by a purpose-made storage unit with mesh screens. This contains the washing machine and all the service control units, and shields an otherwise open-plan shower area. The lavatory is in a cupboard that has two hinged doors contrived to be shut against adjacent partitions even when open, a trick that creates a larger cubicle. Such a device was used by the Surrealist artist Marcel Duchamp in his Paris apartment but for entirely different reasons. Duchamp's door, set in the corner of a room, with one door leaf serving two openings, had written on it: 'When one door closes, another door opens' – which clearly in that instance was not the case, since the door was always shut. Folding screens are also used to surround the shower. The slots between the boards on the American oak floor are detailed, as on a yacht deck, with wide secaflex joints, but in the shower area the gaps are left open to allow the water to be collected underneath in a tray, thereby allowing the floor to be continuous throughout the entire space. The island kitchen unit is also in oak but becomes concrete for the small section that protrudes externally through the opening window unit, where it becomes a miniature herb garden.

Left
Balcony retracted.

Below
Balcony extended.
The kitchen top extends
to form a miniature
herb garden.

Right
The kitchen with
open-plan shower
area beyond.

Above
View of the living
space with the
balcony retracted.

Colonial Cottage Conversion

Sydney, Australia 1999
Burley/Katon, Halliday
100m² (1080 sq ft)

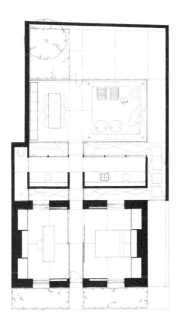

Above
Plan showing the
extension of the original
two-roomed cottage.

Located in a quiet lane only a few kilometres from Sydney city centre, the Colonial Cottage raises important issues about the conservation and extension of historically important small houses. Originally a two-roomed worker's cottage (probably built by a local stonemason for his own family), the house was extensively altered in the late 1980s, leaving only its street façade and simple symmetrical plan intact. The restrictions imposed by the small plot and the planning policies of Woollahra Council meant that design solutions usually adopted for the enlargement of such a property were both inappropriate and unacceptable. However, the radical and inventive idea to put modern pavilions in the rear garden needed the support of a heritage consultant to overcome the planning hurdles.

The original plan form, with two rooms either side of a centrally placed entrance hall, has precedents throughout Europe, from Ireland to Scandinavia and the Mediterranean. This arrangement has been retained and used to generate a clearly defined passage that runs the entire depth of the house – but this is no ordinary passage, for it has a glass floor which is illuminated from below, including the final section that runs into a little courtyard garden with a Chinese elm. From the outside it is virtually impossible to see that the house has been extended.

Opposite page
View along the glass-floored corridor from the entrance hall.

Top right
The street elevation reveals nothing of the conversion.

Right
Sliding panels separate the study and the bedroom from the hall.

Right
Study with moated
lightwell beyond.

Below
Views across
the hall.

Opposite page
The original rooms have
been lined in silver-ash
veneer plywood.

The two original rooms have become a bedroom and a study, both lined in plywood with silver-ash veneer. Large sliding doors open up both of them to the hallway, while their rear windows have been converted to fully glazed doors that lead onto a shallow pool 900 millimetres (35 inches) wide that separates the main house from the first pavilion. At this point in the passage the floor becomes a bridge and the glass walls give side views over what is effectively a moat.

The second pavilion, containing a bathroom, a utility room and a kitchen, is clad in stainless steel towards the old house, and fully glazed to the north, with external blinds for solar control and privacy. These functional spaces have dramatic ceilings 4.5 metres (15 feet) high, and mirror-glass splashbacks in the kitchen and utility room further increase the spatial dynamic. The sunken square bathtub, made of concrete and divided from the external water by a glass partition, is designed to create the illusion of bathing in the moat.

The third pavilion, reached by another bridge over the pool, is fully glazed on its three exposed façades and provides a living and dining space, with the extension of the glass floor of the passage bisecting the space. The jewel-like intensity of this room has been given additional emphasis by the installation of designer furniture – chairs by Marcel Breuer, 'La Chaise' by Charles Eames and a Jean Nouvel dining table.

Right and far right
Views of the moated
lightwell between the
service pavilion and
the living room.

Below
The kitchen uses mirrors
to distort its scale.

Far left
Rear courtyard
is an extension
of the living room.

Left
The living room pavilion
is almost entirely glazed.

Below far left
The glass-floored
corridor is a formal
device to link all
the spaces.

Below left
Furniture by Breuer,
Eames and Nouvel sets
off the architecture.

Houses at La Clota

Vall d'Hebron, Spain 1999
Enric Miralles and
Benedetta Tagliabue
112m² (1210 sq ft)

Right
The new entrance door.

In the right hands, the small house can become a microcosm of the complexity and richness of the natural world. As in nature, over-simplification can be avoided by diversity, differentiation, elaboration, hierarchy and geometry, but allied to this is the need for a vision that allows no single set of ideas to dominate. Architecture, when it performs its historic role of synthesizing the arts, also resists Western materialistic thinking, with its myopic principle of the exclusivity of ideas and theories.

The work of Enric Miralles and Benedetta Tagliabue, in major and minor projects, is a powerful reminder that good art can transcend the confines of particular styles or methodologies. As with their own apartment conversion in the historic quarter of Barcelona, the architects, in converting these two tiny dwellings into one house, have used the opportunity to explore the issue of layering, or over-writing, as in a palimpsest.

Above
Small landscaped entrance garden.

Left
Complex drawing shows both the ground and first floors. The internal elevations and selected details are drawn folded out around the plans.

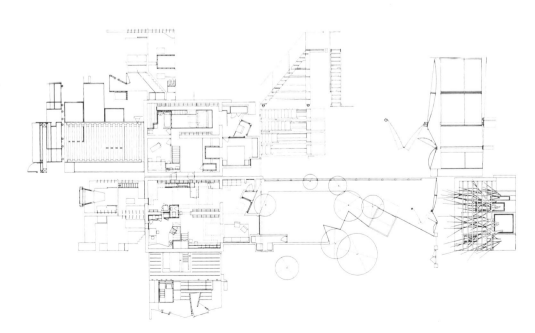

Above left
Double-height study
with mobile stair
topped by a lectern.

Above
View into the new
living area from
within the old house.

The starting point was two adjacent two-storey structures, each hardly more than 3 metres (10 feet) wide. One half retains domestic elements such as the kitchen, dining room, bedrooms and stair, while in the other half the volume has been opened up by the removal of large parts of the original floor, creating a double-height study and library with mezzanine access to the first floor of a small new rear extension. Key features of the original houses have been retained, such as the timber floor joists with their infill shallow vaults, and the rectilinear geometries of the party walls and the old façade to the garden, which has been internalized by the new extension. A former first-floor balcony with ornamental railings has become the new internal access route to the master bedroom. On the ground floor, an opening through the party wall has been partly filled by a new

Right
Entrance hall with landing above. The remains of the old balcony are clearly visible on the left.

lavatory cubicle (conceived of as a piece of furniture), which straddles the gap and provides a visual link between the two formerly separate spaces. Above it, apparently suspended within the void of the library, is the new bathroom.

The library is racked with metal shelving that rises through two floors, with secondary access to the mezzanine provided by a rolling staircase that also acts as a storage unit – rather like a medieval siege tower in appearance, this mobile piece of furniture is crowned by a folded metal lectern. Natural light penetrates the library through a large sculptural light shaft suspended from the original roof. Throughout the house, much attention has been given to the way light falls on surfaces, with walls painted different shades of white, and the floors of oak and bolondo varying in tones and colours.

The external geometry of the small extension combined with the landscaping of the garden avoids the linearity of terraced houses and provides a series of framed foreground views and an entrance that has to be discovered rather than simply approached – like the rest of the house, the front door reveals itself only to those who genuinely wish to unravel its secrets.

Below left
Old balcony abuts new landing – detailing is inventive but relaxed.

Below
The kitchen is partly tucked under the main stair – no opportunity is missed for spatial gymnastics.

Hyperdense Housing at Borneo/ Sporenburg
Amsterdam, Holland 2000
Two houses by Christian Rapp
120m² (1290 sq ft) without glazed conservatory

The development of the peninsulas of Borneo and Sporenburg, on the edge of Amsterdam's eastern harbour area, must represent one of the most radical attempts at low-rise, high-density housing built in Europe since the Second World War. The city authorities demanded a minimum density equivalent to approximately 600 persons per hectare, but market forces still tended to favour houses rather than apartments – and this inherent conflict necessitated a new kind of typology for the basic unit of the master plan. The urban development strategy was arrived at as the result of a competition. The winning proposal by West 8 was a 'Swiss cheese' solution in which 30–50 per cent of the building plots would be void, thereby providing a small patio, courtyard or glazed lightwell. The radical move was to arrange the plots in back-to-back rows within a repetitive party wall system. To aid day lighting of the lower rooms, a ceiling height of 3.5 metres (11 ½ feet) was stipulated for all ground floors. On the first stage of the development over 100 architectural practices contributed to the design of prototypes to be built, resulting in over 2500 dwellings. In addition, a block of 100 plots was sold off to individual clients who then employed their own designers to work on bespoke houses that still complied with the conditions previously established. The result is an environment of enormous visual diversity, surprisingly so given the very restrictive nature of the development plan.

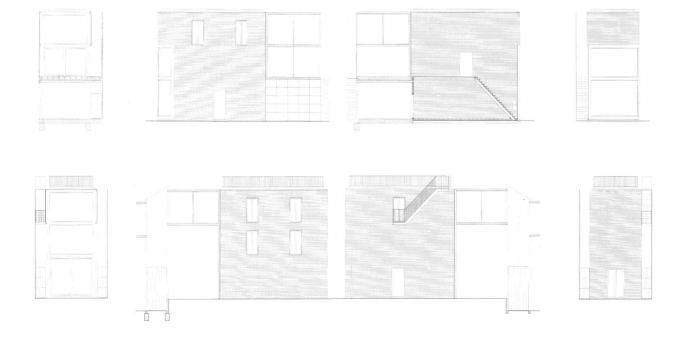

Top
Section and elevations
of number 6.

Above
Section and elevations
of number 12.

Right
Materials are
handled thoughtfully
in the manner of early
Dutch Modernism.

Right
Back-to-back glazed
courtyards on number 6.

Christian Rapp was invited to design a dozen or so dwellings within West 8's master plan, having done previous work in the development of the Eastern Docklands. One of these, numbers 62 Scheepstimmerman-straat on Borneo peninsula incorporates an alleyway which bifurcates the house at ground level – this on a plot only 5.7 metres (18 ¾ feet) wide. Equally radical, number 68 in the same row is a detached house with a gap a mere 200 millimetres (7 ⅞ inches) wide down either side. The two side façades of this house comprise glass or wooden panels that can be opened to allow maintenance of the exterior surface of the neighbours'

party walls. These extreme design responses might be seen as a sign of frustration with the strait jacket of the plot size and zoning restrictions, but Rapp also seems to be searching for some kind of degree zero to which he can return architecture via such modest buildings.

Rapp's later houses on Sporenburg peninsula work with similar ideas but are more authoritative. Number 12 North is a free-standing, three-storey brick box with a partially glazed courtyard to the rear. The alleys on either side are 850 millimetres (33 ½ inches) wide and serve various purposes: an entrance door and high-level stair link to the roof terrace are in one, and the other allows side

windows for additional illumination and ventilation. The plan form seems deliberately contrived to give the house a monolithic and inverted appearance from the street. Number 6 South is end of terrace but still detached. A straight external flight stair from ground to first floor means that the upper part of the house can be used independently. The glazed courtyard is at first floor level with a storage or workshop space underneath accessible directly from the street. An additional stair between the two back-to-back courtyards adds further possibilities for the access arrangements and hence the future functions of the different floors.

Below far left
No 12 is detached in spite of its narrow site.

Below left
Less than 1 m (3 ft) wide alleys give access to the rear courtyard.

Below
Glazing over the rear courtyards form part of the 'Swiss Cheese' concept.

Aluminium House Prototype

Japan 2000
Toyo Ito
109m² (1170 sq ft)

Above
The house is a system
but is specific to its site.

Right
First-floor plan
with sundeck.

Developments in materials technology advanced more significantly in the first half of the twentieth century than in the years following the Second World War. The automobile, the jet plane and the rocket were all prewar inventions that have subsequently been merely refined. The science fiction dreams of the 1950s and 1960s never happened – but the remote stone cottages of the Mediterranean are now less likely to house agricultural workers than weekenders with internet access. The lifestyle transformation of the past thirty years has been largely due to developments in electronics, computing and communications, all aspects of the phenomenon of electromagnetism; our lives are increasingly shaped by the virtual rather than the physical world.

Kocher's and Frey's Aluminaire House (1931) and Aluminium Prefabs (1945) were both examples of experimental projects that took house construction much closer than before to factory production. More than fifty years later, Toyo Ito has revisited this possibility by designing a house made almost entirely out of the material most closely associated with the aircraft industry: aluminium.

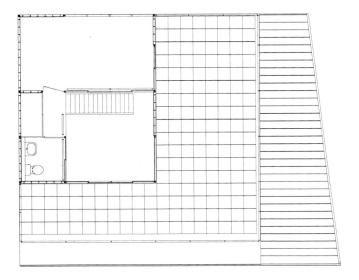

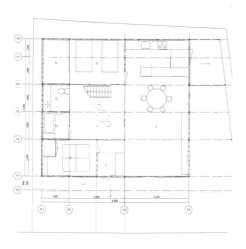

Left
Ground-floor plan.

Below
The house almost
entirely fills its plot.

Above
Main living space
with central atrium
on the right.

Extracted from bauxite, aluminium does not have the best environmental credentials – only 1 per cent of the volume mined ends up as pure aluminium, with the rest being consigned to spoil heaps – but it is recyclable and it can be used for both structural and cladding elements. It is a myth that aluminium is light; volume for volume, it is heavier than concrete, but the difference is that it can be rolled into very thin sheets or sections.

For Ito, the attraction of aluminium was that the same material could be used for the structural frame, the roof, the floors and the finishes, thereby producing a surface unity characterized by that most magical of physical properties – seamlessness. To achieve this, he invented a matrix of cruciform columns with rectangular cover elements that accommodate a variety of junctions involving cladding panels, glazing units, sliding doors and internal partitions. Purpose-made hollow-core I-section beams span these columns and support profiled aluminium plates which form the floor and roof decks. These surfaces are covered by timber and concrete slabs respectively.

The frame is configured into a two-storey structure with the main accommodation arranged on the ground floor around a central sunroom or atrium. Above, reached by a straight-flight stair in this courtyard-like space, are a guest room and a roof terrace. As with many Tokyo sites, the house footprint fills much of the available space; the remainder is used as a car port, shaded by an aluminium pergola.

Implicit in this plan form, with its flexible and forgiving grid, is the suggestion of the many variations that the system could generate. By concentrating on the design of the components, rather than on the finite object, Ito has avoided the reductivism of so many attempts at the mechanization of house building.

Above
Car port with sunscreen.

Above
Most elements
are aluminium.

Above
View across the atrium.

Above
Detailing is very precise.

Urban Village Housing

Edinburgh, Scotland 2000
Richard Murphy Architects
Typical one-bedroom flat
55m² (590 sq ft)
Typical two-bedroom flat
65m² (700 sq ft)

Below left
Typical sections and elevations through the apartment block.

Below right
Site plan with plans of typical units; apartments top, houses to the right.

This development of twenty-two flats and six two-storey houses lies within Edinburgh's New Town, part of the city laid out in the eighteenth century to replace settlements dating back to medieval times. Surrounded by four- and five-storey stone tenements, the new low-rise housing maintains the footprint of what would have been Broughton Village, a small area of earlier timber buildings that partially survived the eighteenth-century redevelopment. The trace of this village, originally surrounded by countryside, has been treated by the architect as a piece of urban archaeology.

Richard Murphy's often stated affinity with the Italian designer Carlo Scarpa goes some way to explaining this approach, for Scarpa's work exemplifies how buildings can be layered to reveal their histories. Murphy's historical references go beyond a building's footprint; they extend to the form language and the specific detail – not as an imitation but rather as a contemporary reinterpretation. Three characteristics of Edinburgh's medieval housing informed all Murphy's significant design decisions on this project: the dominant use of external access stairs, the simple linear pitched roofs, and the lack of formality in the composition of the elevations, in spite of a strong underlying sense of order.

All the first- and second-floor flats are reached by solid masonry stairs, sometimes in combination with suspended galvanized-steel staircases. In the absence of balconies, these stairs provide a place to sit and to put pots of plants. The shallow pitched roofs are made of fibre cement slates, with very slender but deep eaves supported on tapered and exposed rafter ends. At the gables, steel channels support the large overhangs and visually detach the roofs from the walls, so that they appear to float, thereby achieving that most technically difficult of Modernist fantasies – the illusion of weightlessness. The façades are mainly in rendered masonry, with selected areas of cedar cladding at high level and at the gable ends. The junctions between these materials are detailed in galvanized steel, as are the external corners of the timber cladding. Large sliding floor-to-ceiling windows in the living spaces have highly articulated steel balustrades that pay homage to Scarpa's extraordinarily delicate detailing, which approaches the quality of jewellery. Murphy's painterly eye enables him to compose large surfaces so that they never become monotonous or lose their sense of cohesion.

An examination of the floor plans and the terrace sections reveals that all this has been achieved by the simplest of organizational principles – in other hands, the scheme would have been unremarkable. Here, the architecture does not have its roots in one overriding idea but in an accretion of small ideas artistically executed. From a historical perspective, these ideas can be seen to have their place in a recognizable tradition that is constantly evolving.

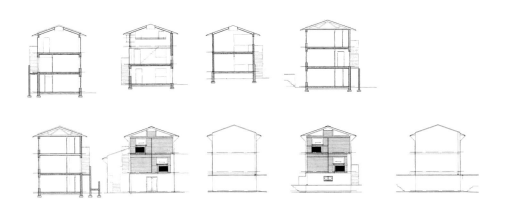

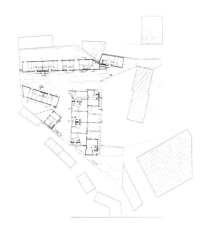

Left
There is no segregation
of cars and pedestrians.

Below
Apartments are
reached by external
stairs which act
as planters and
places to sit.

Above
Façades are
layered to give depth
and complexity.

Top
The arrangement of
buildings follows the
footprint of earlier ones.

Above
Small terraces create
intimate urban spaces.

Top
Murphy is overtly
influenced by the Italian
master Carlo Scarpa.

Above
Carefully detailed
roofs give the illusion
of weightlessness.

Above
Junctions are normally in
galvanized steel sections.

Musholm Bay Vacation Centre

Korsor, Denmark
Arkos Arkitekter
Stage 1 – 1997 / Stage 2 – 2001
1-room unit 37m² (400 sq ft)
2-room unit 64m² (690 sq ft)
3-room unit 95m² (1020 sq ft)

Above and above left
The forms of the living
units are inspired by the
nearby timber groynes.

Right
Typical section.

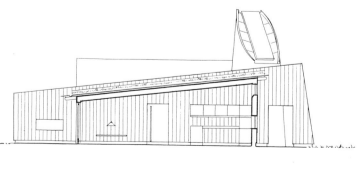

Danish provision of social housing has an uninterrupted history going back 150 years. Since the Second World War, state funding, through long-term fixed-interest loans to housing associations, allied to a stable social democratic political system, ensured the regular building of high-quality architect-designed schemes that remain some of the best examples of public housing anywhere in the world. The relatively small population and the availability of land meant that many of these projects were low-density suburban developments much influenced by the concepts that underpinned the Garden City Movement. The ideas of Ebenezer Howard and Frank Lloyd Wright found a natural home in the Danish landscape. Projects such as Arne Jacobsen's Søholm serrated terraces (1950) and Jørn Utzon's Fredensborg courtyard houses (1964) form just a small part of a highly inventive range of clustered house designs, all of which seek to integrate the built form with the landscape.

The Musholm Bay Vacation Centre stands firmly within this tradition. Providing holiday housing for people with muscular dystrophy, the project was the result of a limited competition in 1995. The new building complex is just 100 metres (328 feet) from the beach and surrounded by cornfields. The competition brief required that all the housing units had a view of the bay with its new bridge connecting the islands of Zealand and Fyn. Most of the houses are arranged in informal terraces on the crest of a hill to maximize the views – they also screen the rest of the complex and form a protective barrier for gardens and playgrounds. Duplex villas are at the perimeter of the site and in the centre is the 'common house', which provides communal facilities. Under a large artificial mound, created out of spoil from the foundations, is an elliptical assembly hall.

The leitmotif for the design is the timber groynes characteristic of the Danish coastline. In both the terraces and villas, the party walls, often not parallel, are taken up above the roofline and out beyond the façades in order to make specific external spaces and counter any sense that the buildings form part of an institution. The external boarding is in local Thuja wood, while the generally conical concrete bathroom cores punctuate the composition at regular intervals. This reflects the construction system, which is sectional timber frame stabilized by the solid core elements. The majority of the monopitch roofs are covered in turf, while the bathroom cores have zinc with integrated solar panels.

In spite of their apparently complex forms, the houses closely reflect contemporary methods of building construction in Denmark, which is highly systematized and uses a large number of prefabricated components. Rather like Utzon's Expansiva Housing (1970), the multiplicity of forms comes from a full exploitation of such components beyond their apparent limits.

Right
The new complex is just 100m (328ft) from the beach.

Far right
Inland, the buildings are surrounded by wheat fields.

Right
Concrete conical
bathrooms punctuate
the composition.

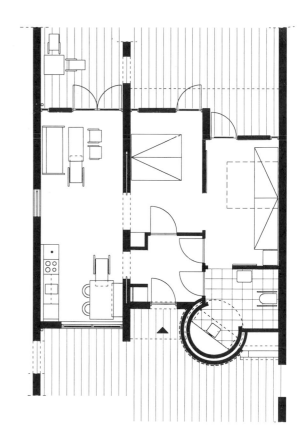

Above
Plan of a typical
unit designed to
accommodate
wheelchair users.

Left
Protected terraces are
created by extended
party walls.

Fred, Su-Si and
Urban Addition
Portable
Housing

Austria 1996 and 1999
Oskar Kaufmann and
Johannes Norlander
18m² (190 sq ft) /
30m² (320 sq ft) /
120m² (1290 sq ft)

Above
Fred being unloaded
from a platform truck.

Below right
Plan with unit both
closed and extended.

Opposite page
Setting the unit up on
site takes just 2 hours.

At the end of the nineteenth century François Hennebique made transportable houses in cast concrete, units that in principle could be mass-produced like any other consumer durable. However, industrialization never brought the prefabrication of entire living units in the numbers that might have been expected. Buckminster Fuller's Dymaxion House (1927) and Kocher's and Frey's Aluminaire (1931) remain isolated experiments. Production of the British prefab of 1945, many of which were made of aluminium, was halted within a couple of years because of the high costs compared to traditional construction. At the same time, the American TVA [Tennessee Valley Authority] system, using mainly timber, was more successful – by 1948 around 25 per cent of all new housing stock there was made from large-scale prefabricated elements. Recent projects by companies such as Ikea in Sweden are designed along the same lines, with a factory-made timber frame – but these are not finished units and, although the weatherproof envelope can be erected in five days, it takes a

further eight weeks to fit the unit out. Therefore, more than 100 years after Hennebique's experiments, Western countries still produce housing in a way that the Romans would understand.

These three portable-housing projects by Oskar Kaufmann are serious attempts to reinvigorate the idea of factory-finished houses in the context of a society in which more and more people are living alone or in flexible relationships that involve informal cohabitation. To make them easily transportable, all the units are based on the size of a road trailer, which restricts their width to less than 3.5 metres (11 feet).

Fred, the smallest, is an expandable room that is 3 x 3 x 3 metres (10 x 10 x 10 feet) in its closed state. At one end is a compact service wall containing a lavatory/shower cubicle and a deep but narrow kitchen top. The remaining open-plan space can be extended by means of an electrically driven sliding end wall that functions like a large drawer. Made entirely of timber, the room can be set up on site in less than two hours.

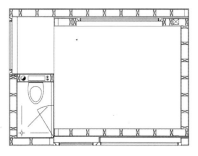

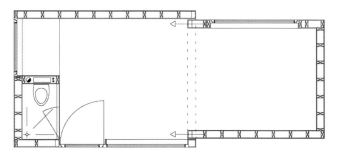

Right
Fred is a truly portable
building and performs
regardless of context.

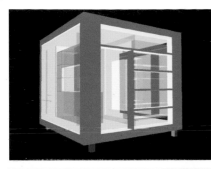

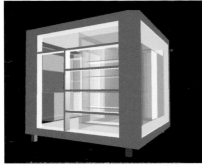

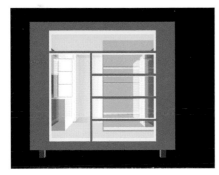

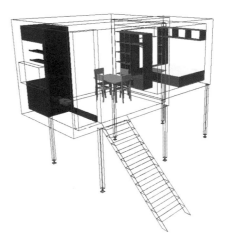

Above
3-D views reveal
Fred's extremely
compact form.

Above right
The interior with
the unit in extended
configuration.

Right
Fred is also
available on piloti.

Right
Elevation of Su-Si Unit,
here shown on piloti
to provide a car port
underneath.

Below
Su-Si is the size of a
sea container and can
be set up in 5 hours.

Su-Si, the size of a standard sea container, is a factory-made unit that can be installed on site in around five hours. At a maximum of 12,000 kg (11¾ tons), the unit can be lifted into position using a standard road crane. Again, the structure and cladding is made of timber, but a fully glazed side wall has been incorporated to utilize the possibilities for solar gain and reduce heating loads. One set of services at each end support a linear open-plan space that houses three zones of occupation for sleeping, living and dining. The unit is configured over a car port and has a first-floor sundeck.

Above
In use as temporary
accommodation.

Right
Plan of Su-Si.

Below
Interior view
looking towards
the sleeping area.

Below right
View towards
the kitchen.

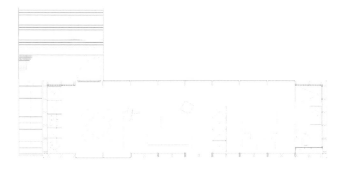

The Urban Addition comprises three stacked prefabricated units with a top deck containing an open terrace and a pool. Manufactured by the Vorarlberg-based company KFN, which specializes in factory-based timber components for the construction industry, the house was designed to suit small infill urban sites. Although each floor has a different function, the units are variations on the same theme, with a narrow linear service core and associated stair defining the basic plan form.

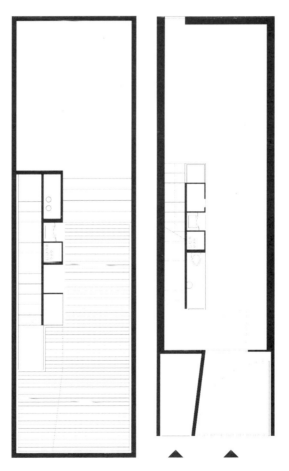

Above
The Urban
Addition interior.

Above left
Typical plans. The
units are intended
for infill sites and
can be stacked.

Tampa Skull and
The Good,
the Bad and the
Ugly prototypes
USA / The Netherlands 1998
Atelier van Lieshout
14m² (150 sq ft) /
60m² (650 sq ft)

Above right
La Tampa is a series of
connected modules.

Sources of inspiration for the work of Joep van Lieshout include the writings of Niccolò Machiavelli and the Marquis de Sade. Both writers were obsessed by how systems could be used to support the exercise of power and the ordering of sexuality. Sade in particular was fanatical about detail, since no deviant activity was conceivable without careful planning and organization. Herein also lies the paradox of Atelier van Lieshout: its architects are subversive at the same time as using the vehicle of art installations, publicity and the props of the very same society that they seek to undermine to develop their work and maintain its credibility.

In the 1980s the studio was concerned with the limits of scientific activity and the understanding that, in science, knowledge can come only from the destruction of the subject through dissection and dismemberment. The furniture produced by the studio in that decade occupied an ambiguous area between consumer durables and art objects. Present in the pieces, which could be combined in different permutations, was the overt suggestion that they represented a new repertoire of sexual experiments. The Master and Slave Mobile Home (1995) changed the scale of this idea to embody whole living units that allowed a nomadic urban lifestyle of self-sufficiency, which was at once critical of and dependent on contemporary culture.

La Tampa is a mobile home originally designed for an exhibition by the Contemporary Art Museum and the University of South Florida in Tampa which subsequently toured the USA. The structure is in four sections of blue polyurethane accommodating a bed space, a dressing room, a kitchen and a bathroom. Each of these minimal spaces has its own external form and is linked to its companions in a manner suggestive of coitus. The usual focus of the domestic environment, the living space, is absent – the implication being that this private retreat is concerned solely with basic necessities, and that all other activities are part of a rural or urban communal lifestyle.

Above
The bed module. Van Lieshout is inspired by the Marquis de Sade.

Left
Each module has a different function.

Above
The violent collision
of different forms is
deliberately provocative.

The Good, the Bad and the Ugly is a larger installation made for the Walker Art Center in Minnesota. Here, a timber-framed shack, lined in shuttering ply, is linked to a modified container unit, in a deliberately perverse reinterpretation of the classic American homestead. Like characters in a William Burroughs novel, the inhabitants of such an environment might well be anarchists, but they never operate without a well-organized tool kit and are experienced in survival techniques, including butchery of livestock (Atelier van Lieshout produce a manual on this very subject). The ordinariness of the building is rendered sinister by its juxtaposition with a mobile space whose function is ambiguous - part workshop, part showcase, part rave venue. Such abrasive projects reveal the archaic nature of most housing design, locked as it is in a historically structured fantasy about the nature of our private lives and habits.

Top
The interior of
the mobile space
is ambiguous in
its function.

Above
Detailing in the
hut is basic but
elegantly conceived.

Since 50 per cent of the carbon dioxide produced in the world comes directly from the built environment, the relationship between buildings and sustainability is a critical issue for the future. One of the compelling arguments for well-designed small houses is that they are potentially very energy efficient – the combination of less built volume and less external envelope means reduced heat losses. This is called energy in use, but there is also the issue of embodied energy – the energy it takes to construct a new building in the first place.

Ecologists argue that we have now extracted enough materials from the earth to sustain the post-industrial nations for the foreseeable future. This implies that everything we use to construct buildings should be made from recycled components and materials – not an impossible vision. Indeed, in the past, reusing timber, roofing slates, stones and bricks was common practice. The medieval builders of Europe often used materials from older buildings dating back to Roman occupations.

Michael Reynolds has taken this idea one stage further by utilizing the detritus of the motor industry to design a construction system that uses car tyres as the basis of sustainable houses called Earthships. In the USA alone, around 200 million car tyres are discarded every year, many ending up in illegal landfill sites. Earthships have their main structural walls made of car tyres stacked and packed with earth,

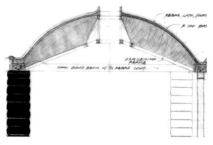

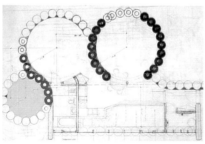

Far left
Section through
living room showing
car tyre walls.

Left top
Plan. The solar space
is at the bottom
of the drawing.

Left bottom
All Earthships have
solar spaces and are
semi-buried on their
shadow side.

Right
Tyres are covered
with mesh and
rendered externally.

then rendered externally. These massive heat-retaining walls are always placed on the shadow side of a house in conjunction with a long glazed façade facing the sun to maximize solar gain. In this sense Earthships have a generic plan and come with tried and tested autonomous energy and waste-treatment systems. But no two Earthships are identical. The Solar Hut is one of the smallest yet built. It forms part of the Gravel Pit Reclamation Project in Taos, New Mexico, and is sited in an area that already has other, larger Earthships, each with individual features.

The plan organization comprises two circular rooms with shallow domed roofs, one a bedroom, the other a living room, linked by a line of service spaces: entrance, utility room, internal garden, kitchen and bathroom. Following standard Earthship practice, these service rooms face south, with glazing set at 30 degrees to the vertical.

The roof of the utility room is a solar panel for water heating, and the room itself contains an array of equipment for self-sufficient living, including batteries that store electricity generated by the photovoltaic panels. The internal garden, which has banana trees, Swedish ivy and geraniums, treats grey water from the kitchen and bathroom, which is then used to flush the lavatory. Toilet waste itself, known as black water, is treated in an external reedbed that returns pure water to the earth. On the west side of the house, and integrated into the plan, is a circular rainwater cistern holding 22,000 litres (4840 gallons), also made of car tyres; this provides filtered water for household use all year round.

For most of the year, the house heats and cools itself passively, but during the coldest months a high temperature burn wood stove is used to supplement heat from the sun.

Top
The dining space with handmade furniture.

Middle
The solar space has an internal garden that treats the grey water.

Bottom and opposite
Detailing is quirky.

In the Grimm fairy tale Briar Rose, a Princess who has been cursed through no fault of her own falls asleep in her castle after pricking her finger on a bewitched spinning wheel. Over the next hundred years a hedge grows up and completely conceals the building and its sleeping inhabitants. On a slightly different theme, in Frances Hodgson Burnet's story The Secret Garden, a young girl discovers a walled garden hidden by plants while staying with her uncle on his lonely country estate in the English county of Yorkshire. Both stories evoke the poetic image of an architecture subsumed by nature, in which the resultant environment is a synthesis of these two oppositional categories. In the eighteenth century Abbé Laugier's idealized primitive hut was in a sense an attempt to find the origins of all architecture in the forms of the natural world. By the end of the first quarter of the twentieth century, Modernism, as a fully developed expression of a culture defined by industrialization, saw architecture as the antithesis to nature. The idea that architecture could be anti-heroic, background, or even invisible runs counter to general architectural practice of the past hundred years, but modest little projects like the Jupilles holiday houses suggest that the ecological agenda is beginning to produce its own aesthetic in which buildings themselves will play a much more subservient role in the creation of places.

Below
Ground- and first-floor
plans with long section.

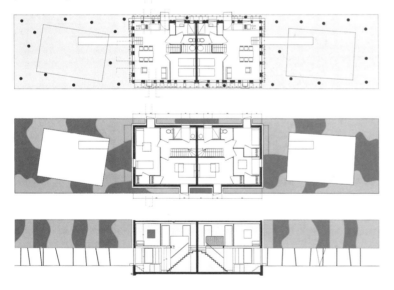

Above
Planting will eventually
cover the building.

Right
Façades have rough-
sawn boards attached
for further concealment.

Top
The living space with
feature fireplace.

Bottom
Deep window reveals
penetrate the
surrounding hedge.

Opposite page
Interior graphics
continue the
forest theme.

The site for this development is adjacent to a forest of mature oaks planted over a century ago, and near to a young replanted forest of oaks just ten years old. The rentable three-bedroomed gites are organized as two-storey, semi-detached houses, each of which is enclosed by a hedge that also encompasses small gardens for each unit. The hedge itself is designed as a thick façade and is contained within a mesh fence at first-floor level with selected windows having deep projections to penetrate the foliage and provide glimpses out of the upper bedrooms. Further concealment of the buildings is achieved through the attachment of rough sawn boards of different heights to the more exposed sections of the elevations. It is clear that, in time, the houses will eventually and intentionally disappear from view like Briar Rose's castle.

To increase the sense of connection with nature, the ground level is banked up around the houses and planted as wild grassland so that this natural landscape appears to extend from windowsill level when viewed from the kitchen or living room. The finishes internally are minimal and made of exposed concrete and untreated timber so that the experience of increasing softness towards the outside is exaggerated. Each house has its own built-in wood stove, fitted within an externally projecting hearth so that the stainless-steel flues sit incongruously between the trunks of the tree hedge.

An existing older house on the site has been converted to provide communal facilities and there is a heated swimming pool which takes up the footprint of an absent house in the rather informal arrangement of adjacent units.

Minibox

Innsbruck, Austria 2001
Hölz Box Tirol
7m² (75 sq ft)

Every summer, large numbers of people in Europe and North America take to the road and condense the requirements of everyday living into a space the size of their bathrooms by living briefly in tents, camper vans or caravans. Some with larger disposable incomes take to the sea in a yacht. In such environments the domestic regime is reduced to a kind of degree zero in which sleeping, eating and personal hygiene take precedence over any other imaginable activity other than sex – which itself, of course, somewhat paradoxically, becomes virtually impossible with any degree of privacy. In our deeply materialistic culture, this dream of escape can only be supported with technology, so that what we expect in a conventional house is still available in a such a space but miniaturized. Historically, this technological provision is a relatively new phenomenon, since before 125 years ago no houses would have had electricity or wash-down toilets, and fireplaces would have been the sole extent of the services. The free plan, that essential ingredient of twentieth-century modernism, was only possible because of the simultaneous development of central heating – the heat source no longer defined the arrangement of rooms.

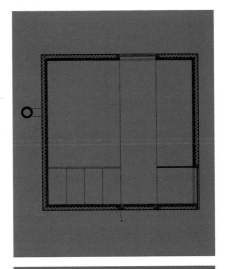

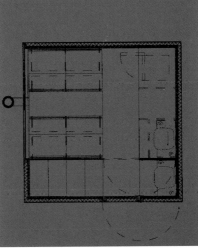

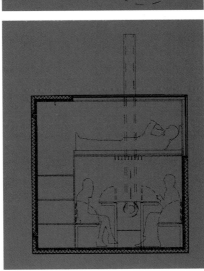

Left
Upper-level plan showing the single and double bed platforms.

Below
This particular installation is on top of a lift shaft.

Above middle
Lower-level plan.

Above
Section.

Opposite page
The Minibox requires very few service connections whatever its location.

Above
The compact space
sleeps three.

Rather curiously, this prefabricated minimum dwelling by Innsbruck-based designers Hölz Box has rediscovered the organizing principle of the fire while at the same time working with an aesthetic based firmly in the present.

The Minibox is a road transportable unit 2.6 x 2.6 x 2.6 metres (8½ x 8½ x 8½ feet) that can accommodate up to three people. Two sleeping platforms, one single, one double, occupy the top third of the cubic volume, the space between them being top-lit by a flush linear roof light. Under the larger of these is the focus of the plan – a dining table under which sits a large wood burning oven that provides both cooking and heating facilities. In the absence of a living room, all domestic routines take place around this table which doubles up as a kitchen. Wall-hung ply benches provide seating and conceal shallow, steel storage trays, while the underside of the bed platform overhead has steel tubes for hanging up pots and cutlery. A storage unit inside the front door also acts as an access stair to the beds. Opposite the table is a bank of further storage spaces and compartments for a camping toilet and shower cubicle. The dimensions allow four Miniboxes to be placed on a standard platform truck and transported to any road-accessible location. A scheme for their deployment as housing for the homeless in the city was abandoned but the units are currently being manufactured as holiday homes, emergency housing or ready-made autonomous extensions.

With their flush detailing and formally composed exteriors, Miniboxes at first display the characteristics of modern consumer durables. In fact they employ timber technology using mainly larch and softwood ply sheeting and depend very little on sophisticated service connections.

Opposite page
The dining table doubles
up as a kitchen.

Apartments and
Houses in Paris

France 2000
Herzog de Meuron
Typical apartment 60m² or
100m² (645 sq ft or 1076 sq ft);
Mews house 55m² (592 sq ft)

The complexity of this urban site has allowed Herzog and de Meuron to employ three of their favoured typologies within one project, each of which they have rehearsed in earlier work but as isolated examples. These three can be termed the screened in-fill block, the long, low terrace, and the individual Ur-form house. The two street frontages of this development fill gaps in the façades of the rue Jonquoy and rue des Suisses. With their dark grey aluminium shutters which en-masse give the impression of a giant hanging curtain of metal, these have their precedent in the scheme for the in-fill apartment block completed in Basle in 1993. It is no coincidence that both Herzog and de Meuron choose consistently to be photographed without any discernible expressions – i.e. with blank faces. In the Paris project, as in Basle, the intention is

more complex than mere neutrality. For as the individual tenants open and fold these shutters, so the façades constantly change and animate the otherwise austere materiality of the surface.

Within the linear inner portion of the site, surrounded by existing buildings, the typology is the same as that used in their project from 1988, again in Basle, known as the 'Apartment building along a party wall'. Given slightly more depth to the site, Herzog and de Meuron have modified this idea with single-storey extensions to the rear of the block that create a series of private courtyards to the larger ground-floor apartments. Like the Hebelstrasse building in Basle, the block is three storeys and shallow, with rooms arranged linearly along its length. In the Paris version however, the

Above right
The street façades have grey metal shutters.

Right
Infill blocks maintain the scale of the existing perimeter buildings.

Opposite page
The linear block has curvilinear timber roller shutters.

apartments have balconies that are protected by curvilinear timber roller shutters. As with the shutters on the main streets, the resultant façade is in a constant state of flux depending on the occupants' need for privacy, shading or security.

Opposite this block, in the inner Isemi-public space, are two mews houses, built hard up against the other boundary wall. These have a strong visual reference to House Rudin, built in Leyman in France in 1997. Like their big brother they have fair faced concrete external walls and simple pitched roofs, asymmetric in this case, which exude a raw quality that alludes to the notion of an archetype. Like the other dwelling units they have shutters on the principal frontage.

The whole complex has been extensively landscaped and planted with trees. A mixture of narrow- and broad-leaved climbers have been trained up specially designed steel cables on the gable end.

Back in 1977, Herzog and de Meuron collaborated with the German artist Joseph Beuys on an installation in Basle, which is where their office is based. Beuys understood that ultimately everyone is an artist and that creativity represents potential, or capital in the best sense. The really intelligent agenda behind this social housing scheme is to attempt to make the position of the architect disappear and to give emphasis to the design as seen from the perspective of those who experience it on a daily basis.

Above right
Planting and landscaping are incorporated into the scheme.

Far right
The shutters produce a constantly changing surface.

Right
The Mews House seen from a private balcony on the linear block.